Praise for TI

"*The Limitless Soul* is a bi... of lives: past, present, future, and life between lives...Practical exercises at the end of each chapter build on the idea of opening yourself up to joy and clarity. Bryn's own unique technique, SESR, is a way to uncover and discover your path on the memory continuum...As a past-life regression-ist for over thirty years, I highly recommend this book as a great way to open up new resources to reconnect with your passion and purpose in life."

—Yvonne Oswald, PhD, award-winning international speaker and author of *Every Word Has Power*

"Bryn Blankinship shares stories of everyday people in this thought-provoking voyage through the spiritual realms ...Through Bryn's clients' stories and hands-on exercises, readers can learn to connect with their soul's wisdom on a deeper level. Reading this book is like having your own spir-itual GPS to help you discover why you're here and unlock the mystery of repeating patterns in your life."

—Samantha Fey, cohost of the podcast *Enlightened Empaths*

"Bryn Blankinship takes the reader on a dynamic journey us-ing hindsight into their past lives and in-between lives, giving them a firmer footing along their soul's path in their current incarnation. This book is enlightening and insightful."

—Lynn Andrews, *New York Times* bestselling author of the Medicine Woman series

"Bryn Blankinship takes us on a fascinating, mind-expanding journey … [She gives us] a glimpse of the spiritual realms of the soul, where, with the assistances of guides, elders, beings of light, and other-dimensional beings, we remember who we truly are, and what we're doing here on Earth. Bryn also offers practical exercises to help us become more attuned to our soul's guidance."

—Carol Bowman, author of *Children's Past Lives* and *Return From Heaven*

"Bryn Blankinship is a wonderful writer and hypnotherapist trained by the maestro himself, Michael Newton (*Journey of Souls*). In *The Limitless Soul*, she continues his research into the between-lives realm."

—Richard Martini, filmmaker and author of *Flipside, It's a Wonderful Afterlife*, and *Hacking the Afterlife*

the
Limitless
SOUL

About the Author

Bryn Blankinship is an award-winning, second-generation hypnotherapist, international instructor, and author. She served on the original board of the Newton Institute as VP/Director of Membership from 2005–2012 and she has been featured in several documentaries and radio interviews on the subject of past lives, life between lives, and Soul Expression Spiritual Regression. Bryn is also the founder of Hypnotic Solutions Hypnosis Center and executive director of the Braithe Center. Visit her online at www.BrynBlankinship.com.

the

Limitless
SOUL

**Hypno-Regression Case Studies into
Past, Present & Future Lives**

BRYN BLANKINSHIP

Llewellyn Publications
Woodbury, Minnesota

FIRST EDITION
First Printing, 2019

Book design: Samantha Penn
Cover design: Kevin R. Brown
Editor: Holly Vanderhaar
Project management: Samantha Lu Sherratt

Llewellyn Publications is a registered trademark of Llewellyn Worldwide Ltd.

Library of Congress Cataloging-in-Publication Data (Pending)
ISBN: 978-0-7387-5888-6

Llewellyn Worldwide Ltd. does not participate in, endorse, or have any authority or responsibility concerning private business transactions between our authors and the public.

All mail addressed to the author is forwarded but the publisher cannot, unless specifically instructed by the author, give out an address or phone number.

Any internet references contained in this work are current at publication time, but the publisher cannot guarantee that a specific location will continue to be maintained. Please refer to the publisher's website for links to authors' websites and other sources.

Llewellyn Publications
A Division of Llewellyn Worldwide Ltd.
2143 Wooddale Drive
Woodbury, MN 55125-2989
www.llewellyn.com

Printed in the United States of America

Other Books by Bryn Blankinship

Memories of the Afterlife
(coauthored with Michael Newton)

Forthcoming Books by Bryn Blankinship

Our Past Lives Before Earth:
The Skills We Bring to Earth

The Topsail Chronicles:
A Spiritual Retreat Meeting Our Guides

To my love, Terry: I am forever grateful to share this journey throughout eternity with you. Thank you for your boundless love, humor, and encouragement.

Contents

Exercise List
Practical Takeaway for a
Soul-Minded Approach to Living

Disclaimer

The information in this book is not meant to diagnose, treat, prescribe, or substitute for consultation with a licensed health-care professional. The author and the publisher do not assume and hereby disclaim any liability for any physical, mental, or emotional harm to any party. Some names and identifying details have been changed to protect the privacy of individuals mentioned in this book.

Acknowledgments

To my parents for their support and vision, pushing me to go beyond my limits.

To Michael and Peggy Newton, for your friendship and our many discussions around the breakfast table, sharing your wisdom and experience.

To my publicist, Devra Jacobs, and to Angela Wix and the team at Llewellyn Publishing, for believing in me and this book.

And especially to my clients, those included in this book and those not. I am honored to share in your cosmic journeys.

Foreword

I am delighted to introduce to you Bryn Blankinship. Her talent as a specialist in the area of previous life exploration led her to develop her pioneering technique: SESR, for resolving current life issues with a deeper understanding of one's true self. As Bryn clearly demonstrates in this classic book, once the positive lesson of a recovered memory has been understood and resolved, it can be released. Enjoy her compelling exploration into previous life case histories, with practical exercises at the end of every chapter to open to your own unique abilities. She is the master teacher and master healer who will bring you home to yourself; the shining light that you are.

The first time I met lovely Bryn, more than sixteen years ago on a Master's Hypnosis training in Virginia, it was one of those rare moments of instant recognition, when two kindred souls were reunited. Of course, we realized during the training that we had originally met in other lifetimes; one in particular in London, England a couple of centuries ago, where, as a widow, I had a respectable job teaching opera to an up-and-coming singer and politician's wife (Bryn!). The Master's training revealed to us that we were both already on our path of personal transformation and self-awareness; our mutual higher purpose was to inspire and transform people's lives in as simple and easy a way as possible. We discovered that both hypnosis and past life work are wonderful and practical techniques for mind, body, and soul metamorphosis.

I had already been teaching past life regression for over twenty years, having discovered Buddhism in my endless search for answers for "What happens next?" after my sister (then eleven) died of cancer when I was thirteen. In Toronto, in my thirties, I worked for more than ten years with the Learning Annex, teaching upwards of twenty-five people in past life groups monthly, as well as facilitating individual private sessions. I found it easy to take people back, utilizing archetypal imagery and breathing techniques that led to strong memories and emotions surfacing from their hiding places in the body. Spontaneous memories would emerge from before conception, to in utero, to previous lives and between lives. My clients always had profoundly moving and sometimes cathartic sessions, which resulted in positive therapeutic changes, both physically and emotionally.

It quickly became apparent to me that memories retrieved during past life journeys were simple messages from the unconscious mind to clear old beliefs or memories that were still active and unresolved this lifetime. The mind uses past life experiences to show what needs to be changed in the present life experience. No matter how much we tried to direct it, the retrieved memory would be simply, "And let me give you yet another previous life example of the same thing you need to change right now!" Bryn independently discovered the same thing and invented her SESR technique to bring her clients to self-knowledge on what to do to clear old beliefs from THIS lifetime, using previous lives and between lives experiences as examples of what *not* to repeat this time around, or perhaps remembering successful lifetimes worth repeating.

Regression is an amazingly effective way to open up self-awareness and free past beliefs. Bryn studied with Roger Woolger (*Other Lives, Other Selves*), an Oxford University graduate and Jungian Analyst, very early in her career. An articulate, kind, and brilliant teacher, Roger's ancestral work revealed how our physical and subtle bodies carry stored memory patterns which can be transformed for resolution of longstanding issues. He also taught how as a person develops, guides or guardians pace the progression of an individual's growth appropriately for that individual. Carl Jung believed that, like the body, the psyche is a self-regulating system. And that a message given by the unconscious mind is always given to you in an easily understandable way, whether through dreams or newly surfacing memories from before birth.

Later, Bryn studied and worked with Michael Newton, PhD (*Journey of Souls*), a pioneer in the field of spiritual regression, who provided insight into the preplanning that occurs for souls with the assistance of spiritual guides prior to incarnating. She continued her studies with Brian Weiss, M.D. (*Many Lives, Many Masters*), well-respected for his past life therapeutic work.

Are past lives real or imagined? The law of conservation of energy states that the total energy of an isolated system remains constant. This law means that energy can neither be created nor destroyed, only transformed. So, life and death would appear to be simply new chapters in a much longer story.

The Great Memory

This vantage point states that there exists a vast universal storehouse of both memories and imaginings that anyone can access freely. The memories can be determined by communication with the unconscious mind though dreams, meditation, hypnosis, or even daydreaming. Carl Jung called this the collective unconscious and the spiritualists and Edgar Cayce refer to it as the Akashic record. Joan Grant simply called it "far memory." The concept does not necessarily require a belief in reincarnation—it's as though there is a vast DVD library of all of humanity's experiences that the unconscious mind can access as an example of what needs to be changed. So, for instance, someone trapped in an unhappy relationship may "remember" a lifetime when they were in prison and would be led to ask themselves, "How am I imprisoning myself today?" This goes along with Rupert Sheldrake's discovery that self-organizing living things (from molecules to entire galaxies) are shaped by morphic fields. They have morphic resonance; i.e., every time we learn something it is passed on to the rest of humanity, rather like a cumulative and collective memory.

Another explanation of past life memory is that each individual is a microcosm of the macrocosm and that we are evolving as a part of a unit of universal intelligence, so memories of past lives are simply a way of helping humanity to evolve on a group level, with the information being passed on to benefit the collective via morphic resonance.

Reincarnation

This belief is that we are born many times over in different bodies to learn new lessons, choosing parents with the genetic makeup that can help us on our journey while experiencing karma, Sanskrit for "action," in which negative action results in a negative reaction and positive action in a positive one. Avoidance does not work. You can choose to walk away from a person with whom you are in conflict, but unless you *truly* let go, you are guaranteeing that you will meet them again under similar circumstances. In the Kabbalah, meaning is given as to why we do not remember previous lives at birth. The angel of forgetfulness touches the lip of the person being conceived so that they are not encumbered with previous memories of lifetimes or confused with the weight of too much information!

One of the most compelling and convincing recent examples of proof for reincarnation is the plethora of surfacing memories from children born after 9/11, who, at around four or five years old, had clear recollections of the towers falling and remembered their original names, which were then found on the memorial plaques in New York. There are some fascinating 9/11 reincarnation stories like these on YouTube.

Whether you believe in previous lives or not, your unconscious mind is like a "quantum internet" with access to all there is to know about you and your existence. The common thread in all previous life interpretations is that the memories produced are not arbitrary; they are directly related to specific patterns that remain unresolved and need addressing by you to clear them so that you can live your life freely and happily.

Go right ahead and enjoy exploring Bryn's interesting, educational, and compelling book!

Yvonne Oswald PhD, award-winning
author of *Every Word Has Power*

Introduction

Many people hold a false assumption that we are all supposed to grow old. The truth is we are all born with a purpose in life; a mission. Some fulfill that mission sooner than others. Regardless, when that mission is done, we are finished and return home, no matter our chronological age.

Why do some people seem to have everything laid out for them on a path to success while others struggle so along the way? Why do some people seem to be able to put their needs first and others seem to be more comfortable taking care of others' needs before their own? Why are some people self-assured and others riddled with doubt? Why are some folks resilient and healthy, living to a ripe old age, while others suffer from illness or even die young? There are no accidents. People are exactly where they need to be in life, doing exactly what they need to be doing, even when it doesn't appear to be so. The lessons are in the interactions, or lack thereof, with those around them. There is learning on both sides—as caretaker or the one being taken care of ... as leader and as follower ... as betrayer and as betrayed.

You were born for a reason. Understanding that reason not only helps make sense of life, it leads to greater fulfillment through a passionate quest for daily living. Without that knowledge, you can be left with a feeling of disconnection or even a sense of loss.

This collection of case studies will reveal the complexities the soul faces by design throughout its many incarnations, and how revisiting certain times in our soul's history can provide insight and release energetic blockages that were impacting our current life incarnation. It is a chapter-by-chapter look at different past life and afterlife cases (which are unconnected and independent of one another) to explore many aspects of a soul's incarnations, showing that life is not a random series of events.

Souls learn with each lifetime they experience. As one spiritual guide stated, "No life is wasted, there are lessons in every kind of life." For example, there are wealthy lives and poor lives where souls experience unhappiness, restriction, and laziness; and there are other wealthy lives and poor lives where souls experience happiness, love, and joy. Economic status is not a measure of happiness or pain.

The exercises at the end of each chapter bring you practical ways to achieve a greater connection with your soul energy. Doing so ultimately leads to a greater sense of inner harmony, self-confidence, and trust.

About Me

I have always been fascinated with the idea of reincarnation; even when I was a little girl I often wondered where we come from. After hearing in church that we had life everlasting and would go on to greener pastures, it left me pondering: if we go on somewhere, then we must come from somewhere, too. I was left with more questions without answers. Without knowing it, I had laid the foundation for my career as a hypnotherapist, helping myself and others find the answers to these questions and more.

I came to this work unexpectedly. I was on the East Coast pursuing my dream of being an actress, and I sought out a regressionist for a past life session to clear what was holding me back in my acting career. One past life regression turned into a future progression, which gave me glimpses into future events I would experience. I saw myself standing in a field of prairie grass, looking out over the hillside. There were trees metaphorically holding "apples" that represented gigs that were to come. I was told that I would go to Los Angeles for one reason, but it would change into something else while I was there. I didn't know what that meant at the time, but I knew I had to go to figure it out.

All the pieces fell into place when, not long after the session, I got a call from an actress friend living in Los Angeles. She encouraged me to come out there, so I did. After arriving in LA, I enrolled in an acting class, and soon signed with an agent. I began auditioning for whatever I could and within a short period of time I booked commercials and had a few smaller parts in films.

Through a series of events, I found myself on location in an area north of LA called "the Grapevine," standing in a field while filming a commercial. I had my own dressing room with my name and star on the door. It felt magical to be there! I stepped out to look at the view over the hillside when someone warned me to be careful of snakes. I looked down at my feet and up again, when I suddenly had a flashback to the future progression that had led me to LA. I was standing in that same field with the prairie grass and the trees that I had been shown glimpses of; it caused me to think about the interconnectedness of things.

I loved LA and had a blast auditioning, booking gigs, and meeting up with my friends afterward to share audition stories. Then one day it struck me that it was time to move behind the scenes. The years I spent in LA were instrumental. Having moved beyond my own personal limitations, I knew I could help others with theirs using hypnosis and past life regression. I found the interconnectedness of things even more amazing as I thought of all that had transpired to get me here. I also realized I had come out to LA in search of a dream but found something else I could bring home that I was equally, if not more, passionate about.

This led me to begin training in a new career as a hypnotherapist and regressionist. I was so excited to get to learn how to do this and immersed myself in learning all I could! While still in LA, I took hypnosis training and, after returning to the East Coast, I sought out the best regressionists in my field for training.

I have been fortunate to have studied spiritual regression with many of the great teachers in this field. My early training was with Roger Woolger, Michael Newton, Brian Weiss, Henry Bolduc, and others. With each one I learned the most amazing things. I am so grateful to have had the chance to learn from them then, because as of this writing, many of them have moved on to the afterlife themselves. Now their work will live on and evolve through their students as they assist us from the cosmic realms.

I found a kindred spirit in Roger Woolger, who is known for his therapeutic ancestral work for accessing and clearing sense memories stored in the physical and subtle bodies and accessing the spiritual realm, referred to by Buddhists as the bardo state. I was on a study track with Roger and this fascinating work when I discovered Michael Newton.

Michael Newton was a remarkable teacher and his Life Between Lives Hypnotherapy course answered the many questions I had about a soul's preplanning with guides prior to incarnating and review after an incarnation. The bigger picture was starting to make more sense to me. This left me at a crossroads; whether to continue with Roger Woolger or learn more from Michael Newton. It was at Roger's next course that he encouraged me to keep learning and suggested that I teach.

Just over a year after taking Life Between Lives Hypnotherapy Certification with Michael Newton, I was asked by my colleague Paul Aurand to help Michael and others launch The Newton Institute for Life Between Lives Hypnotherapy (TNI). I served on an interim board before becoming VP/Membership Director and an international lead instructor. It was with Paul's support that I stepped into my role as teacher—for the institute and for my own hypnosis practice.

We went on to build an international organization with members in over forty countries. I served as a board member for seven years, as well as an international lead instructor, before stepping down from the board to focus on my own work. And in 2014, two years after leaving The Newton Institute, I was honored to receive the Peggy Newton Award for Outstanding Service.

The years I spent at TNI were an important step in my journey and I appreciate the support from Michael Newton and the camaraderie with my colleagues in this emerging field of mindful exploration. It was during this time that I also met and studied with Brian Weiss.

Michael Newton remained a dear friend and mentor. As synchronicity would have it, we regularly saw one another when I was teaching my certification courses near where Michael and his wife, Peggy, lived up until his passing. We'd reminisce about the early days of the Newton Institute. I treasure the time I spent with them and hold those memories close.

It's important to note that my father had a lifelong interest in the power of the mind to overcome obstacles and maintain wellness in the body. He certified in hypnosis many years before I did, focusing on self-hypnosis. And it was my mother who encouraged me to follow my dreams to see where they led. As a second-generation hypnotherapist, I come to this work naturally, though I took an indirect path.

Doing this work, I had found my true calling! Teaching the Hypno-Skillsets and Past Life Hypno-Regression certification courses I've developed to my own international student base gives me great satisfaction, as I help others overcome challenges and connect with the innate wisdom within themselves. I started doing Life Between Lives Spiritual Regression sixteen years ago. Over time, my sessions shifted from my original training as my own work evolved into what I now call All Lives Regression and Soul Expression Spiritual Regression (SESR).

About this Book

The clients in the cases used in this book came for SESR sessions to gain insight into their soul's intention and earthly lessons for their current incarnation. This book is about clients finding and following their soul's guidance, and includes exercises designed for the reader to begin the process of awakening to soul. The stories are taken from session recordings, notes taken during the session, and follow-up notes afterward. Stories in this book are based on hours of session time. During this time, clients often deliver long, rambling passages filled with rich insights from guides; I have paraphrased these for clarity and condensed them down to the chapters in the book.

In writing this book, my clients' names have been changed and personal details left out to protect their identity. I have also chosen to leave out their soul names, soul colors, and guides' names, because these are intensely personal to them. Where guides' names are mentioned, they have been changed. Names and places have been verified for accuracy where possible, and sometimes those of famous people and places in a past life were left out, so as to not detract from the deeper message of the story. Famous or not, they are just souls incarnating to have the experience they needed.

What is Soul Expression Spiritual Regression?

This work developed over time from my own training and experience in past lives and Life Between Lives when I saw an opportunity to expand this work to enhance the soul connection. Soul Expression Spiritual Regression is a transpersonal hypno-regression technique for accessing the soul level of the mind. A SESR (pronounced *sessor*, as in "assessor") session offers a review of one's current life, which permits the magnification of one's soul in the current mind and body. It allows one to identify and review the past and future simultaneously from the perspective of the current life, with direct guidance from one's soul and spiritual team for clarification of one's current life purpose. Armed with insights regarding one's strengths, weaknesses, and progress to this point in life, one can resolve current life issues affected by karmic carryover and move forward with greater clarity, joy, and peace for restorative balance.

Simply put, a SESR session is an assessment session that allows clients to review and assess their current life status midway through a lifetime, rather than at their death, when it is normally done. By making connections at the soul level of the mind, a SESR session helps clients find and follow their soul's guidance, identify negative patterns, and move through their issues more quickly. This saves time; the client avoids having to be born and start all over again to complete lessons.

The soul is the link between the human and Source. In order to be in unison, there must be a meeting of both the human self and the soul self. SESR opens this connection at the human level to the presence of one's soul self, which resides in each of us; here, an energy transfer takes places that strengthens that connection for direct communication with one's soul and spiritual team. During this process, the client lifts their energy vibration to a level that increases communications with guides and one's soul, as guides lower their own energy vibration. The communications take place in the middle where the two meet. SESR is about connecting with the soul self and bringing those attributes more fully into your human expression.

SESR shifts the focus onto bringing in soul energy and shifting the subtle bodies for a recharge and magnification of one's soul expression in their current incarnation. This knowledge provides soul guidance and alignment to aid in achieving one's purpose faster and better.

Too often people set an intention and when it doesn't unfold immediately or in the time they expect it to, they change their focus to something else before it's able to come to fruition. The seeds of intention must be nourished with thoughts of desired outcomes while taking actions toward that end. They must be given time to grow, along with flexibility and inner guidance in knowing what direction to go in. Through SESR's personal assessment and its energy work, clients can learn to look at their current life with a new perspective. It's a chance to look at issues and identify them in their current life to shift what needs shifting for a deeper understanding of one's true self.

Prerequisite to SESR

Prior to experiencing a SESR session, clients have had at least one past life or All Lives Regression with me. "Past life regression" is too limiting and is not truly an accurate term, since lifetimes are not necessarily lived in a linear order. I've developed a technique called All Lives Regression, which I use to prepare clients for SESR; it allows clients to access *all* lifetimes, past and future, to find the one(s) that hold the answers they need to bring resolution. Revisiting another lifetime serves as a tool for gaining insights and healing old wounds to get the most from the current life; this fosters the client's growth along the way. The life you're in is the important one.

With regard to future events, clients can be shown glimpses of potential future events, but the future is not laid out for them. They must find their way forward. Clients have free will to choose to do something or not. There are no absolutes.

What makes SESR different from traditional Life Between Lives Spiritual Regression is the method used to access the spirit world, and how the time is spent in the spirit world. In a typical Life Between Lives session, clients are regressed through their current life, into the womb, and into a past life. The past life death scene serves as the entry point into the spirit world. In SESR, clients are given the option to go directly into the spirit world, bypassing the womb and past life altogether, so that more time can be spent in the spirit world. Information regarding a relevant past life is often given by guides later in the spirit world without taking the client through a complete past life.

The SESR model evolved with each client, and was developed over the years as my clients began bypassing certain areas of the spirit world that were interesting, but not always necessary for them to visit.

Why Do Clients Seek SESR?

Many cultures recognize the immortal existence of the soul and its incarnations into various bodies and lifetimes. They access this wisdom with the help of shamans, psychic mediums, and seers who possess special abilities to tune in on behalf of the client. SESR allows the client this direct access to themselves.

My clients come from all walks of life, with different belief systems regarding life, politics, and religion. The common thread that joins them all is their belief in something more than this current physical life, and their desire to know more about the role they play in it. They come from all over the world for SESR sessions, yet their findings are consistent with one another, regardless of nationality or religion.

Most seek out a SESR session for one of the following reasons: to find and enhance the connection with their soul to better follow their soul's guidance while in this current incarnation; to make contact and strengthen communications with their guides; to discover more about their current life's mission and what they are here to do; or to find peace and possibly make contact with loved ones who have crossed over.

No matter the path that led them to my office, clients desiring a SESR session are seeking answers and understanding while living this earthly existence. They find comfort in knowing that they are not alone, but have assistance along the way from their spiritual team, who are there to help them succeed. These sessions provide insightful awareness that allows them to put worries and concerns to rest, to find peace, and to move forward feeling more empowered with the understanding that they were born with a purpose and that there is no one who is just like them, even identical twins. Every soul is unique!

What Happens During a SESR Session?

A SESR session is three and a half to four hours long. It is preceded by an All Lives Session of about two hours on a different day to prepare the client, getting them used to working in a deeper trance state. A few clients choose to do more than one All Lives Session before having the SESR done.

Clients are guided into a deep meditative state using hypnosis techniques. Each client's experience is unique. Some clients travel to places in the spirit world, while others get the information through conversations and interactions with guides. Clients tend to describe similar areas or groups, which I refer to as "Soul Reflection," "Soul Awareness," and "Soul Advisory Council." (Please refer to the glossary at the back of this book for a description of terms used in the stories.) Clients may visit

Soul Reflection, where they are given glimpses into significant lives (past and future) that hold relevant information to their current incarnation. The client's spiritual team—consisting of guides and Soul Advisory Council—give input as to their progress. During this process their guides come through as intermediaries for the client to assist them and provide guidance. As this happens, clients communicate telepathically with their guides and then share with me verbally what is said. Often while in this meditative state the soul, a guide, or sometimes a member of the Soul Advisory Council speaks directly through the client to me. When this happens, the client is still present and aware of what is being said. Their voice changes from their natural speaking voice and they speak about the client in the third person.

One's state of readiness and ability to let go are important factors in accessing the wisdom within. Everyone comes to these sessions with different experiences and varying levels of awareness. This is not something that's done "to" a client. They must be open to the experience and actually participate in it. Everything one has done in their life to this point can either assist (or hinder) access to this place deep within.

Clients experience a great deal in the session that is more than can be put into a few words. In the stories that follow, it's important to note that not all clients are "visual," although the stories may read that way. A visual client "sees" images or scenes during the session, an auditory client "hears" the information, and some clients get information kinetically, through "feelings" or a "sense of knowing."

In this deeper state of hypnosis, one can create a channel for communication to align with the soul. Upon emerging from this deeper state, clients are free from karmic entanglements and left with a greater sense of clarity about their current life purpose.

Practical Takeaway for a
Soul-Minded Approach to Living

What does it mean to be soul minded? It means knowing that we are more than the flesh and bones that make up our human self, and that we are connected to our own spiritual team on the other side who assist us along our earthly journey. Knowing this brings comfort, but there's more to it than that. Your soul knows what you need, and it is available to you when you know how to listen and connect to it through intuitive awareness.

You can ask for help and when you know how to look for the signs you can "know" to navigate your path more easily. It begins with getting "quiet" and turning inward.

In session, clients are given messages from their guides that directly relate to them. There are other messages that have dual meanings that relate not only to that individual client but also to humanity and our human existence. Exercises at the end of each chapter offer practical applications for you to begin learning the soul-minded approach in your own life (be sure to do these in a safe place and never while driving). These exercises are to help you with finding and following your own soul's guidance.

Emotions such as fear, jealousy, shame, and guilt are lower level energies that sit densely on the physical and subtle bodies. Shifting your thinking away from them and onto higher energies like love, joy, and happiness enlivens the subtle bodies with vitality and openness to intuition. Each exercise is designed to clear and lift your energy vibration to bring more joy into your life as you strengthen communications with your guides and soul.

How You as the Reader Will Benefit

I have found myself personally touched by each and every one of my clients, which has, I hope, made me more understanding and compassionate of their plight in life. It has also given me insight into events in my own life, knowing we are not alone; there is a guiding force underneath it all. I hope that by reading these stories you will feel this, too.

I share on the following pages as a way of being authentic to what transpired during these deeply profound sessions. Statements made by guides on such topics as politics or religion are not meant to be for or against any one group, but are important to give perspective on matters that can help one understand why some things are as they are. It is my hope that you will find the accounts in this book helpful in some way and find peace in knowing that life is eternal and the soul lives on.

chapter 1
Struggle, Justice, and Beliefs

Early on in my teaching career a funny thing happened. As I sit quietly observing a pair of students at training who are facilitating their first afterlife sessions, I suddenly get a sharp pain on my left side around my abdomen. It grows sharper and sharper until I can't breathe. I signal over to the training assistant and quickly leave the room. Once outside of the session room, I stand for a few minutes using my breathing to release the pain. It is so odd, but I can't shake the feeling that I had just been stabbed.

My side starts feeling better, so I pull myself together and go check in on another student pair who are doing their sessions in another room. I quietly open the door and go in. The student who is facilitating the session is sitting behind the desk, while her partner, John, is lying back in the recliner absorbed in a scene from the last moments of one of his past lives. I stand in the corner quietly observing them when the pain returns even stronger now.

I hear John quite matter-of-factly say, "He killed me … he stabbed me! I'm dying. I stabbed him too … but I didn't kill him."

John continues to describe the scene of his death on the battlefields at the Battle of Antioch during the time of the Crusades. As one of the Knights Templar, he wore a white mantle with a red cross, and rode a horse with a red tassel on its head. His hair was long, and his beard was now encrusted with a mixture of blood and snow.

It was cold and snowing, and their army was running low on supplies and manpower. As they came up over the horizon there were thousands of Turks prepared for battle, waiting to take them by surprise. The Turks swarmed upon the invading army and attacked. The young knight brutally battled his way through the sea of men and found himself engaged with one Turk in particular. Bludgeoning one another, the knight was finally knocked off of his horse by his adversary. While his maimed body was lying on the ground, his Turkish attacker jumped off his own horse and continued to stab him, making sure to finish the job.

As a young man the wounded warrior had looked forward to growing up and becoming a knight, as did most of the young boys in the village. He had been taught that to go to war on the side of Christianity was to fight for justice and for God. Now approaching thirty, he was wiser and weary from many battles and saw things differently. Disillusioned, he now believed all this fighting was nothing more than an exercise in power and greed. Stealing from one thief to give to another.

But once "in service" there was no way out. He knew that he faced certain death from his own army if he were to speak out or try to leave. He had seen what happened to those who had tried to leave, so he kept quiet and did what he had to do, no longer out of loyalty to any belief, but out of a sense of survival until these fatal wounds offered the only way out of this lonely existence.

And now he was dying, feeling angry as if he had been tricked into service along with other young men just like him. Giving his life for something he no longer believed in, he welcomed his death and his freedom.

As his soul leaves the lifeless body, the facilitator carefully guides him through the death scene, asking him to bring forward those he had loved in his life. He struggles as he looks back over that life; he had no one... no one he loved or who loved him... except for his horse.

"The closest thing you have is your horse who's with you in battle," he says. He describes his life as a knight as a lonely life of solitude. There was no special someone to go home to. Even if there had been, it doesn't matter because he hasn't been home in so long he doesn't even know where that is anymore. All he has now is his horse and what he carried with him.

So, he musters up courage after feeling the intense loneliness of the life he had just lived, and looks into the eyes of his horse, thanking him for always being there and then he lets go. His soul is gently taken to a special healing place to be cleansed of the emotional imprint that this particularly difficult life has left on his spirit.

This doesn't seem out of the norm to me; in fact, I recognize much of the scene he is describing. Months prior to this day, I had facilitated a session with John at my office before he had even decided to take my hypnosis certification course. The battle scene from the Crusades, the white mantle with the red cross, and the red tassels his horse wore all seem familiar to me in great detail, as if I had been in the room watching their session the entire time.

As John comes out of the session he seems so shocked at the depth of loneliness and isolation he feels from that life that he hasn't yet realized that I have joined them in the room. I give him a moment or two before speaking and then ask, "Don't you recall we went to this same scene when you came to see me at my office last winter... the battle, the red cross, and the horse with the red tassels?"

He very clearly states, "No, we didn't go to this life in that session. This is the first time I've ever revisited this life."

I reply, "Yes, don't you remember the weather was harsh and you were so weary, but you had no choice but to fight?"

He insists, "Nope, this is the first time I've revisited this past life."

"But how would I know all of these details when I wasn't in the room with you today until the very end of your session?" I argue. "I was held up with your classmates' session down the hall."

I then turn to the student who had just facilitated the session and ask if she had remembered to ask if he recognized the person who had stabbed him to death. My reasoning for this is twofold. First, soul recognition occurs when a client recognizes someone from their present life who appears in their past life, so it's important to ask. Second, it is an opportunity for healing if forgiveness work or grief work is needed, or if there's conflict or unfinished business to be resolved with them.

She starts to speak when she is interrupted by John, who looks up at me and points. "Why, it was you, Bryn. You're the one who stabbed me!"

Then they simultaneously say, "Bryn, why are you holding your side that way?"

I look down and realize that I am holding my side, which has started hurting again. Startled and laughing all at the same time, I say to them, "A few minutes ago down the hall I had to leave the room because I suddenly had the inexplicable feeling that I had been stabbed!"

We are quite surprised once we all realize that the reason the details of the battle scene from John's session are familiar to me is because I had been there myself. Although it's happened once or twice, I don't typically end up in my clients' past lives. I know the scene not from having facilitated a session or as the observer, but because I had lived it along with him.

I know this to be true also because I began to recall one of my own sessions that had occurred during the Crusades, but I had only known about a small portion of that life from when I had popped into a different time frame in that lifetime. Now years later, John's session fills in some of the blanks for me from that life. It also reveals a connection to John, whom I had not met yet in my current life at the time of my session.

John smiles and says, "Don't worry, I forgive you. I was only thirty years old but was ready to be done with that life. It was a painfully lonely existence." He feels a lingering sadness at having such difficulty in finding someone to say his goodbyes to in that life and after several moments of searching, all he found was his horse. As he lets go of that life, almost immediately the pain in my side goes away too.

Not every death is over and done with without animosity, but for that lifetime that's what it was. John and I have no unfinished business to work through. He simply needed a way out of that life, which I unknowingly obliged on the battlefield that day as a worthy opponent.

In a follow-up Soul Expression Regression Session (SESR), John discovers more about his life's purpose helping others as he crosses into the spirit world, and his guide greets him and takes him to another realm, to a city in the sky. From here John is led to a facility where he is greeted by a priest who has knowledge and an understanding of how things work. The priest informs John that we come to Earth to learn. "In order for our soul to develop, we must understand truth. There are those on Earth who have come to foster truth. This is an interesting experiment. We are looking to see whether we can shift the consciousness away from where it has resided for a long time. How much of a shift can we make based on souls who have incarnated to battle the illusion and pursue truth?" he says, as he reminds John there are forces of good working in the world too.

The priest begins to perform a sacred ritual with swirling light in front of an audience who is participating to send support and love to the earthly realm. He explains to John that this needs to be done to help with Earth's transition. "We do this to combat the dark, the lower dimensions that influence the Earth realm," he says. "We can then learn to communicate truth in a realm [Earth] that doesn't like truth or want to hear truth…Earth is a school with a certain way of doing things. This realm is one of duality. It is not pure, it is not truthful, but it is buried beneath the distractions or physicality of this realm. It is there for us to discover. That is the learning here. Many believe they have truth, but they have beliefs. Beliefs and perceptions are not truth. You have to discover truth on your own. When you discover it, you know it. This is a battle. Without what we do, Earth would be very dark. The more people that are awakening on Earth will tip the scales. This is the duality."

The priest reminds John that this city in the sky is the place that he returns to between lifetimes. "In the spirit world, we have many other existences. Many roles we play," he says. "We will prevail; we always do."

He reveals to John that in his current incarnation, he is doing residual work to help others open to truth. "Souls can fall off their life path and learn but is this the right learning?" he asks. John helps others to see beyond the material world of competition and possessions that can distract souls who incarnate on Earth, causing them to lose focus of why they are here. It's okay to have material things, but when that's where the focus is, it puts one on the wrong path of learning. He reminds John of the importance of souls staying connected to the divine.

The priest explains, "You have to begin to understand what the Earth realm is, and your soul will develop to a higher level and you'll have more opportunities open to you. This work is to get the individuals to do the spiritual work we do to accelerate the rate and the pace of the development."

His final message for John is, "To know truth, you must seek out truth. Truth can come incrementally, and the path may have detours. It's not a straight line, especially on Earth."

John feels recharged and happy as a result of his visit "home." In his current life, he has a strong dislike for injustice and dishonest practices perpetuated by corporations, governments, religions, and other organizations that operate merely to keep people in the dark, or as an exercise in greed. These beliefs have carried over from that lifetime a mistrust of people who used the system for their own political power and gain, as well as other lifetimes in which John was responsible for keeping law and order. In one life, he died as a lawman following his duty to uphold the law and keep order and truth in the untamed Wild West. The warrior life carried over into John's current life, causing him to be passionate about righting wrongs by helping others see through the deception that's being presented to them. It's about aiding humankind in finding truth.

—— *Soul-Minded Journaling* ——
Identifying Your Beliefs

Where are you struggling in your life? What beliefs or concepts are giving you difficulty with regard to society's expectations or your own beliefs about yourself? Are you feeling disillusioned or do you feel empowered and hopeful by what you see around you? Are you able to cut through illusion and see truth? Is it difficult for you to move forward with goals you've set for yourself? What beliefs about yourself are holding you back from achieving your goals?

1. Reflect on your current situation to identify your beliefs about yourself and the world around you by pondering some of the questions above.

2. Now, reflect on your past.

   • What childhood/early adult experiences shaped these beliefs?

   • Have your beliefs changed or have they stayed the same throughout most of your life?

3. As a result of those past beliefs that have shifted:

   • Have you become more open, or more closed off, in your interactions with others?

- Are you authentic or hiding behind these beliefs?

- Has this benefited you or become a detriment to goals you've set for yourself and the relationships in your life?

- In hindsight, do you see them differently than you once did?

4. What goals have you set for yourself?

- What is holding you back from achieving them? Starting them? Finishing them?

- If you could have what you want, what would that life look like?

5. Ask your spiritual team for guidance. You can ask your soul directly, or ask a spiritual guide who is a member of your spiritual team.

Sit quietly with your hand over your heart. Relax your breathing. Bring your attention inward. Ask your soul or spiritual guide for guidance. Listen to what is being revealed through messages, feelings or intuition.

As you learn to discern the ways your soul or guide sends guidance, notice when things flow and when they seem blocked. Notice how you "feel" when you follow your intuition or know you're moving in the right direction. Learn the difference between "feelings" and the gentle nudge or warm feeling you get when your soul is naturally guiding you through intuition. Learn what it feels like when your guide is sending guidance.

Practice this regularly to learn to find and follow your soul's guidance, and to discern the ways that guidance is revealed to you in your life.

chapter 2
Experiencing Restriction to Understand Freedom

During pretalk, Valerie shares with me some of the health issues that had forced her to leave her job several years before. In addition, her boss, who had been an antagonist to her, had made her job situation even more difficult to deal with. Valerie wants to explore with SESR to gain more insight into this situation.

As we began the session, Valerie moves backward in time through a series of happy childhood memories to a time where she and her sisters are playing in their playpen. Wearing their pajamas, the girls climb, jump, and laugh together in their living room. The session continues back to the time before birth through her soul's history to the year 1852. Valerie describes being dressed in an ornate silk kimono with a rich red, black, and green pattern overlaying a white background, and wearing black silk sandal-like shoes. Her face was painted white with accentuated lips and eyes, and her black hair was swept up into three buns made from her own hair and held together by adorned combs and sticks. She wore the formal dress of a geisha.

She was seventeen years old and her entire life to this point had been dedicated to training to become one of the honored geisha. As a *maiko*, a young apprentice, she had lived in a geisha house owned by her master, Chin-Yung. He frequently told the girls it was an honor to be learning the geisha tradition, which was known for service, music, and dance. He often reminded them how special it was to be called geisha because not every girl who trained would become one. She dutifully took pride in learning service without question, hoping she too could one day be one of these special women. She excelled at the art of making tea.

At last her dream was realized, and she became a geisha along with a select few others. It was then that she learned that in her master's geisha house, as part of her servitude, she was expected to provide sexual favors for wealthy men who would be chosen by Chin-Yung. Upon discovering this, she felt a part of her rise, wanting to rebel, but years of training had taught her she could not. She wanted to warn the younger girls who looked up to her now, but there was no point. There was nowhere else to go, and this was the only life she had ever known. She realized how naive she had been to be enticed by the seeming beauty of these women, the way they moved and dressed, without looking deeper into all that it involved. The beautiful clothes, hair, and makeup made her feel special to be noticed by men. She had not truly understood what it meant to give men pleasure until she was forced to do it.

Just a few months prior to turning seventeen, she had been taken aboard a large boat by Chin-Yung, along with three other girls she had grown up with at the geisha house. They were told little about what lay ahead for them. The boat stank and there were smelly sailors who stared and pawed at them. The girls were instructed not to speak to anyone or one another and, as expected, they did as they were told.

The long boat ride took them to a foreign land with strangers who did not speak their language and customs they did not understand. They landed in America where men wore black pants with a jacket overtop a vest with a pocket watch secured by a chain. Chin-Yung quickly adapted to this style of dress and added a hat with a rounded brim to make him appear like the rich American bankers and other wealthy businessmen in town to whom he planned to peddle his wares—the girls.

The displaced girls were given their own rooms with rich fabric and traditional Japanese décor. These living quarters were located above a saloon in the heart of San Francisco, which was frequented by wealthy local businessmen. Chin-Yung had instructed the girls to not speak to one another as a means to control them, so they wouldn't try to run away. They were locked in their rooms and only taken out one at a time. Meals and men were brought to them. They were given herbs to make special waters for cleanliness between servicing clients. Some, who paid more, stayed with the girls for an evening, while on other occasions they had several customers in one night. Because of her looks and especially her demeanor, Lo Ming [Valerie] considered herself lucky to be mostly reserved for wealthier men who could afford to stay longer. It was the lesser of two evils.

She had been called "slut" and "whore" so many times by her master that she had forgotten her given name. One of the regulars had gotten Chinese and Japanese mixed up, and came up with the name Lo Ming, which he called her, and which she now answered to. It was a sad existence for her. She felt betrayed thinking that being geisha was special, now coming to realize that here the title meant nothing more than being a glorified prostitute. She was locked in a room all day with no freedom and if she was lucky, she was given a meal and a basin of water to clean up with.

Although there was a window in her room that overlooked the streets of San Francisco down below, her training was deeply ingrained in her. She never called out or tried to escape because that was not acceptable and besides, even if she had, no one understood her language and she didn't understand theirs.

She had experienced her master's temper during times where he would grab her around the throat or shake her tiny body violently. For a moment she had the thought of fighting back, but then her training would kick in and she'd remember her place of servitude. Besides, if she did manage to get away, she had no personal belongings other than her kimono. She had no money and nowhere to go.

It was in this moment that soul recognition occurred and Valerie recognized her master Chin-Yung as the current life boss with the fiery temper who often tried to manipulate Valerie to do things that were unethical. When Valerie refused, she felt the brunt of her boss's anger directed toward her in retaliation. Emotional—rather than physical—browbeating left Valerie feeling powerless to fight it, so she held it all in, recognizing this was her employer she was up against. It was during this intense time that her health began to decline significantly. Ultimately Valerie decided her only defense was to get away from the situation by leaving her job, which was something Lo Ming wasn't able to do.

Lo Ming's sad, long days were spent in this room watching people living their lives. She could see them walking along the boardwalk—some wealthy, some poor—kids running, and horses pulling up to the mercantile across the street. Her afternoons were spent preparing for clients, the rich men who she would service until the early hours of the morning. The next day only brought more of the same.

Time passed slowly for Lo Ming, seeming like an eternity as days turned to months and months to years. Now at just twenty years old, she found herself lying in bed locked in the same room that was all she had known these past three years in America. She was sick with fever and her stomach hurt, and she was there all alone. No one had checked in on her for days now. She began to realize that she was in labor, having a baby—but that something was going wrong.

Isolated in this place, she had no medicine and no other women who could even explain to her that she was even pregnant. Only the awareness from her higher self's perspective revealed what was happening to her now. She had not known about such things because it was not discussed with the younger girls, and since becoming geisha, she had been in a foreign land and kept locked alone in a room. She hadn't had access to the right ingredients that were native to her home in Japan for the special waters she had been instructed to use between clients to prevent pregnancy.

As the contractions continued, she screamed out, but no one came. No one cared. As her belly had swollen, she had still been required to service the men, especially the fat banker who had taken a liking to her. He paid her visits more than the other men and was most likely the father of this child. As she screamed her last scream, she felt a gushing sensation between her legs and then she died.

Lo Ming died immediately. "Poor little thing" was the final thought she had of the infant she was leaving behind; "free at last" as she thought of herself. As the soul leaves Lo Ming's lifeless body, making her way home, she is joined by the soul of the baby girl who had died moments after Lo Ming. Their two souls return to their eternal home in unison, taking parallel tracks to the spirit world. They wave goodbye to one another upon entry into the spirit world knowing they will see one another some other time.

Upon being welcomed home, a guide appears, explaining that the baby's soul had been brought in to help Lo Ming find her escape to freedom through death. Knowing it would not survive the birth, this soul agreed to come in with the sole purpose of getting Lo Ming out of that awful life. The two souls are in each other's lives today and are very close.

After this initial meeting with her guide, Lo Ming's soul is taken to a healing place to recover from the sadness and despair of the life she had just lived. Much of the session is actually spent here to release the sticky residue of that difficult and painful earthly life. She is guided through a soul recalibration process to restore her energy.

Afterward, during Soul Reflection, Valerie reviews the life with her guide, who helps her to understand that the primary purpose of that lifetime had been to experience a life of restriction and living under someone's thumb, so that she could truly understand what it means to be free. The contrast of experiencing hardship and to also experience easier lives shows the difference between the two. "Every incarnation offers a gain; there is no loss," she shares. "What we as humans think is difficult is not; it's in our minds. Souls know this, but the human mind gets in the way."

In choosing the life of a geisha, her soul experienced restriction, and in her job with her boss, she did too. Valerie overcame it in the end—once through death and once by leaving her job when the emotional distress became physically crippling.

Her guide adds that holding in negative emotions for prolonged periods forces them to find an outlet. They eventually manifest in the body as illness or pain. Tears are a way for the emotional body to pull up the stuck emotion from the body. Tears can be therapeutic and serve as a release for the emotional body and the physical body. It's important to learn ways to manage one's emotions. Emotional health is as important as physical health.

The session had a profound effect on Valerie. Working through the emotional life of that past life brought insight and resolution to her current life situation. Since the session, previous emotional restraints and physical symptoms have lessened tremendously. Insightful awareness gained with the aid of her guide has allowed her to release the pattern of being entangled in servitude. She recognizes how she can now help others to get what they want, but without having to give up her own needs or be forced to suffer in order to please others in the process. And she has a new perspective and appreciation for her life that have led her to a new career path helping others with what she's learned through this experience.

—— *Soul-Minded Exercise* ——
Healing Balloons

What areas of your life cause you to feel disconnected from your spirit or disempowered? Identify the heavy feelings you carry that cause you to feel restricted in your life. What has been on your mind that it's time to let go of? What issues are you seeking resolution to?

Visualize a bag of special healing balloons in various colors.

Now imagine taking those disempowering feelings and breathing them out, into the healing balloons, filling as many balloons as necessary until you begin feeling a sense of peace and calm come over you. Imagine letting go of those feelings and thoughts as you fill these balloons. Notice the colors of your balloons. Do the colors hold significance?

Now taken a nice deep, cleansing breath and with each exhalation imagine releasing those balloons off into the horizon into the light to be transformed, no longer to be an issue for you. Notice how much better you feel letting those things go.

Now take those good feelings and allow them to fill the spaces where you once felt the hurt, sadness, or anxiety. Write down any insights you feel as a result of this.

Now that you're feeling lighter and have lifted your vibration having let those negative things go, enjoy feeling more present and empowered in your life, making room for a deeper soulful connection to help from the other side.

—— *Soul-Minded Exercise* ——
Affirm, Ask, and Align

This exercise is for gaining clarity and strengthening the ability to find solutions more quickly and in alignment with the guidance that's available to you. It's to help you change the way you look at your life by developing a sense of appreciation for what you've got, as you move into future goals and desires.

1. **Affirm what you have.** Journal about the people, skills, relationships, and things that you appreciate in your life. The way in is through the heart and not the head. Don't overthink it. Mean it when you say you appreciate it.

2. **Ask for guidance from your soul/spiritual team on what you want help with.** Get clear on what you're asking for. Accept that help is available to improve the situation, and that it is possible. Recognize times in your past when you felt connected to the flow that created past desires you have already achieved.

   If you have doubt or resistance, embrace it as a learning tool to explore where the root of this doubt or resistance stems from. Go back to the Healing Balloons exercise and release the doubt, replacing it with trust. Trust that help is available and be open to what's possible.

3. **Align with the solution as you allow it to unfold.** Sit or take a walk as you actively envision having this come to you in the flow of divine timing. Let your imagination play with what it looks like and feels like to have these things happen. Allow it to come "through" you from your heart and soul (and not from your head/thinking mind). Be flexible with your vision, adjusting it as it unfolds. Imagine it as if it is occurring in the present moment. Repeat this often throughout your day.

4. **Act on the guidance you are being shown,** one step at a time. Look for signs, such as gentle nudges, number patterns (on clocks/odometers), or symbols with special meaning to you that cross your path. Notice chance meetings, opportunities, or experiences that cause you to light up and bring you joy.

chapter 3

Grieving Loss

Martha chose to have a SESR session after the sudden death of her daughter, who died a violent death at the hands of a deeply troubled individual she knew. After her daughter was shot, she lingered for a few days before the life left her body. Her friends and family were terribly saddened by these events.

It has been a couple of years, but Martha's heart is still filled with great grief from the loss of her daughter. Martha wants to know her daughter's spirit is now at peace and is curious if she has tried to communicate with her. She is also left with questions surrounding the events. Understanding there is a deeper connection to the others in her life and in the spirit world, Martha wants to discover more about her connection to her daughter and with her guides. I tell her I will do the best that I can to help her find answers to her questions, but that I can't promise anything other than to assure her that she'll get what she needs from the session.

Martha's initial session is a particularly challenging one because she gets images and information but then her analytical mind tries to explain it all away, creating interference. This can happen sometimes with clients when they are doing this work for the first time and, in Martha's case, because she is working through the additional layer of grief.

As she crossed into the past life, Martha became aware of blue skies over snowcapped mountaintops on a sunny but cool day. She was a man in that life, herding goats along a rocky mountain peak that had patches of green growth where the snow had melted. He was holding a staff which helped him keep his balance as he moved along this mountainous terrain and through gnarled trees that grew out of it.

Life was simple here. A plain, wooden lean-to provided shelter to shield him from the weather at night. It was quiet and there were no others around. He wore a brown cape with fur to keep warm. His modest boots were not leather but were made from animal skins and tied up his leg.

Each day was similar to the next, herding goats along the grassy areas and allowing them to graze there. He occasionally went to the trading post down in the valley below. Here he traded skins and goats' milk for provisions that he couldn't make himself.

Our session ends here. Although the information that came through is somewhat cryptic, it will prove to be very important. Martha agrees to rest that evening and come back the next day for the SESR session.

The second day, the session flows more easily. Martha is more relaxed. She now knows what to expect and is more comfortable with the entire process and has let go of trying so hard. She decides to just let the details come through however they come without the pressure she put on herself the day before to immediately understand it.

She went into a past life in the early 1920s and Martha again was a male. In this life, he oversaw the building of the railroad along a coastal area near a major shipping port. The landscape revealed shrubbery, palm trees, and tall, white, contemporary buildings along the waterfront. There were boxy black automobiles parked about. The exact location of this place was not revealed but he was an American working for an American corporation that had a joint venture overseas to expand marketing efforts.

We learned more about the life, but most days were like the last. At the end of it there was an overall sense of pride in having accomplished something important. Upon leaving the body, the soul immediately crosses into the spirit world and is greeted by a loved one from Martha's current life who had died a few years back. Her loved one now leads her over a sloped, wooden bridge and onto a shiny, wide walkway, which Martha laughingly describes as looking like celestial wet cement. The walkway then opens into a vastness of white light.

After a long journey through a Gothic stone archway up a hill, a male guide dressed in a robe stands waiting by a gate. He takes Martha through a series of little rooms that she describes as being equipped with "celestial medical equipment." They stop in one particular room where her guide picks up a large white protective sheet and wraps her in it. She feels it sending energy to her. She becomes aware of a soothing, energizing white-yellow light moving through her, lifting the heavy load she carries in her heart, and her spirit, from having lost her daughter. She begins crying, surprised by her own tears.

The session ends after a long period of energy work with her guide. Her list of questions is not addressed, at least not in words. They are perhaps something to look at for another time. Leaving my office, Martha looks content and there was a peacefulness in her eyes.

A few days later, I receive an email from Martha about something interesting that had happened after her session. She writes that when she was setting the GPS system in her car to return home, she was puzzled at first by the fact that it had mapped out a route along a two-lane road through the countryside and small towns, instead of the interstate highway it had used to direct her to my office.

She chose to dismiss the urge to go back the same way she had come, and decided instead to see where this new route would take her. She set out for home, relaxed and unhurried, driving through stretches of rolling hills and green countryside. After a while something caught her attention. To the right of her was a herd of goats and a goat herder!

Smiling, she circled back around just so she could pass him again. They waved at each other and she continued on her way home. She felt that this was affirmation that her guide was still with her hours after the session, and a validation of her experience. It was no accident that the GPS had purposely led her along this route to reveal the goat herder to her!

Martha also mentions that since her daughter's death, she has become accustomed to driving without music playing, preferring the quiet and her own thoughts. On the way home, as she was packing the car, she noticed a music CD in the trunk; she had not listened to it in years and had even forgotten what was on it. She decided to play it on the ride home.

She felt uplifted by the music. What stood out were two very meaningful messages that came through in the lyrics of the songs. The first song, "Don't Stand by My Grave and Weep," carried a message about her daughter, letting her know it was time to let go—a timely reminder to Martha that her daughter's spirit had not died but had transitioned into the spirit world.

The other song, "Hold Me Angel," served as a message for Martha to trust that her guides are with her always, even during the difficult times she has faced. It reminded her of the white protective sheet her guides had wrapped around her in the session to bring comfort to her. Martha knew she was not alone and could turn to her guides to guide her through this period and that things would be okay.

—— *Soul-Minded Exercise* ——
Grieving and Forgiveness Visualization

Are you grieving the loss of someone due to a change in the relationship, or their actual passing? How are you experiencing that loss? Do you have feelings of intense sadness, blame, or anger toward someone as a result of their leaving? Do you have lingering unanswered questions that keep you locked in thought and keep you from moving forward in your life?

Imagine yourself sitting on a bench. Across from you is another bench where the person you miss has come to join you. They may be living, or they may be deceased. Connect to them wherever they are and have a conversation in your mind, to share with them the feelings that are in your heart.

- If this is a loved one who you miss having in your life: share with them the things you enjoyed about them or doing with them. Keep their memory alive by remembering the good times. Feel the good feelings as you remember them. Let this fill the space in your heart with love.

• If this is someone who hurt you: let them know how the things that they said and did affected you. Let them know that you're not going to let this stop you anymore but that you are just letting them know. Release them and let them go.

Reclaim your power from these situations so that you can be more present as you move forward in your life at this time, knowing that although they are not in your life anymore or have completed their earthly journey, you will see them again at the appropriate time.

Learn to recognize in the stillness that you are not alone. Feel your spiritual connection being strengthened.

—— *Soul-Minded Exercise* ——
Sound Healing

Music and sound are healing. Certain beats are uplifting.

Do you listen to music regularly? When's the last time you stopped everything for a while and just sat and listened to your favorite music or artist? When you're doing chores around the house, do you turn the music on in the background? While you're driving on a road trip, do you turn on music?

Do you play an instrument? If so, when's the last time you played? Chimes and drumming can shift your mood too.

There are different kinds of music for different things. Let the music take you to another place. Let it shift your mood. If you're sad, play sad music to get it out. Play joyful music to lift your vibration. Play music that reminds you of loved ones or close friends. Let the music shift you to a higher place.

chapter 4

Taking the Path
of Contemplation

Jason and I have worked together a few times over the years. He is seeking guidance through a SESR session to learn more about the patterns of things and some of the decisions he's made that have brought him to this point in his life; he knows that they came from a place that was "bigger" than himself. He is curious about what lies ahead, and wonders how he can pass on spirituality to his children without going to a formalized church.

Regarding patterns, Jason has an interest in numbers; he is also curious about how the "taste of things" can evoke such strong memories. Jason owns a chain of pubs. Sometimes, while going through his daily routine, he experiences flashes of past lives, like when tasting certain foods or stirring a pot of food. His children also remember previous lifetimes related to foods and events, such as being Japanese and sipping tea in ancient Japan.

Jason's guide takes him through a series of lifetimes that are relevant to the bigger picture Jason is curious to explore. Following is one of those lifetimes with additional significant messages from his guide during Soul Awareness.

After crossing into the spirit world, Jason's spirit passed through a wooden door, rounded at the top with wooden bars. He recognized his surroundings to be medieval times around the 1300s in France. There was a long table laid out with round metal trays piled high with fruit and bread. The walls were arched and cave-like, resembling the inside of the lower level of a church. Oil paintings covered the walls. The room was dimly lit by only the light streaming in from the high windows above. This church-like place felt familiar to Jason and he commented that it reminded him of the décor in his pub in his current life.

His name was Brother Henry and he was a monk. This sect held the common belief of service and contemplation as part of their religious practice, though they were more lighthearted than other sects.

Brother Henry served his brothers and the village as a bread baker for the monastery. A wooden table in the kitchen held bowls of grains that provided the ingredients for Henry's bread recipes. He baked the bread in a large wood-fired oven. Henry was meticulous with his bread recipes and enjoyed spending time baking different kinds of breads and then analyzing it to perfect the recipes. He especially appreciated the wonderful, yeasty smell of fresh baked bread. A favorite meal of Henry's was a chunk of aged cheese, which they also made at the monastery, served with a fresh piece of yeasty bread.

On this day, delivery day, horse-drawn carts loaded with supplies were waiting on the cobblestone streets outside. Brother Sal was helping with the unloading. It was nearly eleven o'clock in the morning. Nearby, other monks, who are dressed in dark gray-brown robes with hoods, began gathering. Their hoods were up, signaling that prayer time was to begin. Brother Sal continued to unload the carts in preparation for lunch once prayer time was over, while Brother Henry went to gather wood for the fire.

On the way to collect firewood, Brother Henry passed by what he called his "thinking tree." It was situated at the point where the street to the village intersected with the path from the monastery. Although he found pleasure in the solitude of spending time under this beautiful, sprawling oak tree that had a calming effect on his spirit, there wasn't time for that today. Fortunately, he could pass the thick, solid hardwood on the way to and from running errands. A glimpse of the tree would have to suffice for today.

As he passed the tree again on the way back with the wood for the fire, Brother Henry thought for a moment of his dear friend Brother Sal and how not only were they good friends, but they worked well with one another in the milling area. With just the two of them there, they often joked and were lighthearted. They let go of the traditional formalities and didn't always call one another "brother" like the other more serious-minded monks adhered to so, when they did, they laughed about it.

Henry returned to the kitchen and placed the wood on the fire. He observed that prayers were about to start. "Time to get serious," Sal commented. They put their hoods up and gathered up their books. As they enter the gathering room upstairs, Sal joked again, "Why can't they make these seats more comfortable?" Henry observed to himself there were too many monks and not enough room on the bench.

As one of their brothers led them through morning prayer time, Henry looked down at the cross etched on the front of his Bible. It was burned into the leather cover. Henry thought for a moment of how he had tried to learn leatherworking upon first arriving at the monastery, but he didn't like it. He much preferred working with the bread instead. Making bread was his "useful purpose." His mind quickly returned to the prayers he and the other monks spoke in a mix of French and Latin.

It would be lunchtime soon. When prayers were over, the brothers would all exit out of the gathering room and go to the dining area downstairs to eat together at the long table with the long bench. Another bench with too many monks and not enough room on the bench, Henry mused.

Henry shared again how this sect was more lighthearted than a typical monastery. This abbey was part of the village and unlike many, it had its own stables. The breads they baked and cheeses they cured were not only to feed the monks but were also traded with the farmers in the village. They traded bread, cheese, and grains for fruits and vegetables they didn't grow on their own. Henry and Sal knew how to pick out the best fruits, despite the farmers trying to pass off the worse ones in trade.

To supply the monastery with water, the monks bottled mineral water they got from the creek that ran through the village. The mineral-rich water had medicinal healing properties. The village was famous during this era for having the best water.

Later that day after lunch, Henry left to go to the village to purchase more milking cows for the monastery. Although the city was not far away, Henry preferred the peacefulness of the village. Riding along with his horse and cart, Henry enjoyed

this little excursion. As he rode through the village he identi-
fied the shopkeeper's daughter, the tailor, and the blacksmith as
people he knew in his current life.

This time on the way back to the monastery, Henry had
time to stop and sit under the thinking tree for a bit. This tree
provided a place of quiet contemplation for Henry that was
separate from the place the monks gathered for prayers. In the
solitude, he could "feel" the energy of his family there.

Henry sat under the thinking tree, at first fondly remembering the good times with his family. His mother's nurturing, loving nature became almost palpable as he recalled the taste of
the fresh jam with figs and rich butter that she used to make for
him because she knew how much he loved it. Henry remembered fun times playing around with his younger brother when
they were kids, before the terrible accident that had killed his
brother. Just two years apart, they had been close.

His memories of his father were mostly of his harder,
denser, downtrodden energy. He worked hard delivering coal
to provide for his family. They didn't have an easy life, but they
were happy together. Soul Recognition revealed several of the
monks, Henry's family, and the boy who was responsible for
his brother's death as people he knows in his current life.

Over the years, Henry had spent a great deal of time rumi-
nating under this tree about his life prior to entering the monastery. He had even built himself a bench to sit on there. He
would ponder things like the loss of his younger brother, and
the death of his parents of the plague just a few years later.

This tree had been Henry's refuge, his anchor of sorts as he
sat there trying to release the anger he felt over the senseless
loss of his brother. It needn't have happened were it not for the
actions of the other boy. His brother was helping his friends

train a spirited horse when one of the boys provoked the horse and was mean to it. The frightened animal kicked and then trampled Henry's eleven-year-old brother to death.

After the accident, it had been difficult for Henry to see his mother in such pain at losing her son and he was devastated at losing his only brother. His mother was sad and cried a lot, while his dad, more stoic, held his feelings inside. The bond between Henry and his mother grew deeper over their shared loss. However, her grief had diminished her energy and she had nothing left to fight with when the plague spread through the village not too long after. Henry lost both parents and his friends in the village to the plague.

At sixteen years old, with nothing keeping him there, Henry left to go to school. He lived in the city for a short time. After finishing his religious training, he joined the monastery. It was his anger toward the boy that had caused his brother's death that had brought him to the monastery.

Over the years, Henry sat in quiet reflection under the thinking tree. It was his solo spot where he had time to reflect on all that had transpired. A myriad of thoughts convened there at that tree. Here he could smell the mineral smell of the spring water; its sulfuric waters felt healing and cleansing to him. Henry loved watching the clouds from his tree, commenting that it was the one constant from life to life. Although he didn't understand the reason for his brother's death, he had managed to find peace with it.

The scene moved forward to many years later in Brother Henry's life. A fire swept through the village causing him to leave. Henry now served as a deacon in a small church not far from the monastery. As a church elder he had more interactions with the parishioners than he did at the monastery.

Henry found a new contemplative space in one of the hallways off the side of the church. The crimson-colored glass windows reflected off the beautiful artwork that lined the hallways. The energy here felt similar to the spot under his thinking tree.

Brother Henry lived out the rest of his days there. He died peacefully, feeling he had fulfilled his useful purpose and his agreement to serve. He was content knowing he had learned to overcome anger through the power of contemplation and quiet thought. As his spirit leaves his body, he is optimistic as his spirit knows there is more than just this life.

Upon entry into the spirit world, Henry's spirit is met by a loved one whom he describes as an angel of energy. She is very happy to see him, and they are very close to one another in her current life. A female guide named Jharisma joins them. Her name is a combination of "charisma" and the "J" from Jason's name, representative of their partnership with one another. Jharisma's energy is gentle, yet feminine, and she hugs them both. The hugs between them are uplifting for Henry's tired spirit.

Jharisma takes him to a place with no physical walls for Soul Reflection. There are wispy, glowing clouds and swirling round energy lights here—akin to the northern lights on Earth—served to enclose the space. She discusses with Jason how in that life as Henry, he was given the challenge of anger and then worked to conquer it. At this point, Jharisma begins speaking to me [Bryn] about Jason as if it were just the two of us having a conversation about him. "I gave him the challenge of anger and then watched to see how he would handle it. Each life I give him a different challenge," Jharisma says.

This often happens in session when clients in this deeper state begin to channel their soul, their guides, past life persona, or even Ascended Masters, who come through to assist the client. The client, although fully aware of what's being said, begins speaking about themselves in the third person to me.

Jharisma further explains: "Choosing the life of a monk was about how to take the anger and have the ultimate challenge of self-contemplation … people can take anger many, many ways and carry it through many, many lives. It can be a good force or a negative force." She is proud of Henry for rising to the occasion and overcoming the challenges he faced.

Henry's life had been a fulfilling one. "Every life we try another challenge and use these to learn from …" Jharisma adds, "As with every life, our energy and things are carried forward. We pick up skills to make the next life better, this is how we measure growth … with each successive life, we determine what needs to be worked on."

Jharisma goes on to explain that each life is grown from the previous life; whether it's food appreciation or how to healthfully deal with anger, even joking with friends, it compounds and passes on to the next life. The friendships, his senses, and the tastes were some of the most enjoyable things about that lifetime. These had been in sharp contrast to pain and anger he experienced due to loss of his family.

Jharisma reveals that Henry's sense of taste was more developed because he slowed down more in that lifetime than in other, busier lifetimes. Jason understands why he readily picks up on tasting patterns and how flavors take him back somewhere.

In the Soul Awareness area, Jason learns more about the interactions with his soul group. Jharisma works with his soul group on how to keep moving forward with the direction of their energy based on experiences from their incarnations. One of the members chimes in: "What do you want your soul to be remembered for?" Jason responds, "There's basic good or evil.

Some souls choose to be remembered for evil. Mine definitely wants to be remembered for good!"

With each life, souls take bigger leaps. Soul growth happens down in the bodies, while processing the lives happens above in the spirit world with one's spiritual team. The more souls grow and expand their core purpose, the more they're able to break through human-made bindings of the life, brain, and bodies they're in. Even with a handicapped body, souls can accomplish great things. The experiences of the bodies strengthen the soul.

Jason's soul group leads with soul. Since it's easier for the body to overpower the soul, the tenacity of the "old" souls helps younger souls strengthen the balance. With so many "younger" souls presently incarnating on Earth, the old souls have to work harder to achieve this balance to keep the younger souls from destroying themselves. There's no room for hatred when leading with soul.

Jharisma reveals that there are several tiers within soul groups. The members of Jason's soul group are deployed often. As a group they explore living dual lives where they play support roles for one another or they can "meet up" when they sleep to foster each other's growth. Jharisma advises that Jason can remember more from this when he awakens if he is mindful of it.

Jharisma addresses Jason's questions about patterns. She helps him to understand that patterns and numbers are the same. Numbers are a way to clarify, measure, and recognize patterns. Although it's thought that humans only use part of our brain, it's more accurate to say that we only use part of our soul connection to the brain. The brain needs to measure and quantify what the soul already knows. Jharisma uses the example of humans' natural connection to ancient sites, such as the pyramids and Mayan ruins, to show Jason how this connection comes from the soul's knowing without having to quantify, but the brain needs to measure and quantify. She adds that the computer was invented as a way to measure what the soul already knows.

Using "soul power," not "brain power," allows patterns in the world that are created from plague, illness, or war to be shifted by a soul correction that takes place. These are needed after these "purges" take place on Earth. The new souls are created to make up that gap; however, it puts more work on the older souls to keep the balance.

Also, fear patterns created by dictators and other treacherous leaders can cause the younger souls to get rooted in the hatred and fear. Jharisma reminds Jason that not all old souls are necessarily good. Some choose evil and actually lead others toward it. Other times they simply get carried away and take things further than what is needed. "Evil" souls return to the spirit world after their incarnations and go through their own process with their soul groups.

Although it may seem that "evil" souls make big change, there are other ways, too. Part of Jason's soul's purpose during incarnations is to seek out other thinkers with open minds and open hearts and bring them together to assist in change. He doesn't lead change as a physical leader, but rather leading the energy that effects change through open, thought-provoking discussions. Jason is advised to "seek out the thinkers and the spiritual will flow." Jharisma reminds him that "all religions have elements of spirituality, but man made them." When you put the spiritual thinkers together, things will fall into place.

During further exploration regarding the incarnation process, Jason is given details of how the soul enters the body. The placenta serves as the entry point for the incoming soul. Inside the womb, the placenta is a shining, glowing power force that serves as an entry or exit point for the soul. The incoming soul enters through the gut, where it's anchored, and then goes up in the body in the shape of an internal light saber with a sheath around it. The soul has a helix (spiral) shape to it, like a continuation of the umbilical cord, that runs along the spine the length of the abdomen to the third eye. The soul force resides there encased in a ball of energy that starts at the gut just below the belly button (the base) and runs up to the third eye (the tip) of the light saber.

Jharisma reminds Jason that he's here to hold a big snowball of light energy. He throws these energy balls like energy forces that explode and open people up. Like a positive mushroom cloud of energy, it enlightens them. She tells him he'll recognize who to throw them to by the light. "I'll know by looking into their eyes," Jason says. "The eyes don't lie." Some of them are members of connected soul groups and some are not. Jharisma says it's like a soul correction by empowering them with a little "recharge." The snowballs of energy he throws to others are similar energy to the light saber, the light force from them is meant for people who need a little recharge.

Jason learns the secrets of how to recharge; there's a silent way or a nature way of recharging. The silent way is to turn your attention within. The nature way of recharging happens by looking up into the trees and into the sky. Standing on the ground and looking up through the layers of trees blowing in the wind opens the energy from above, while the tree roots are grounding.

He's aware of the responsibility these gifts carry. It's not to be wasted, it's to be used. Through experiences earlier in his current incarnation, Jason has planted his rock-solid roots which give him the balance needed to hold the energy of change for many souls because his roots are firm. He has the added soul connection with Jharisma, who comes to nudge him when necessary. Jason remarks, "It's as if she's able to get in and briefly take over the controls."

Jharisma is not there all the time but comes to share energy with Jason to lift him so he can share with others. Her presence gives it intensity. She describes it like airplanes that connect for refueling as needed. She gives Jason a sample of how it feels when she's charging him up, so he'll recognize it more easily in the future when she's there. As she does, he feels a sensation running along his internal light saber.

As the session comes to a close, Jason is advised to take the "contemplative course" when dealing with his current life. He is to make sure he protects his space and finds a thinking tree no matter where he is, because that's the anchor that brings him back. He also has an appreciation of water from that lifetime that he carries with him in his current incarnation.

After our session, Jason smiles as he shares with me that his chain of pubs is named after this lifetime as Henry. Nestled in the mountains, it's a great place for enjoying a heavenly brew. As a result of our sessions, he's begun to recognize the surprising ways his past lives display themselves, for example by things he finds himself drawn to that don't have current life reasons. He also sees his connection to his family, community, and nature as ways of sharing spirituality without the need for a formalized church.

—— *Soul-Minded Exercise* ——
Thinking Tree Meditation

I have had several special trees in my life that I enjoy sitting under while I contemplate life. I return to them in meditations and connect to the energy of that place. One in particular was by a lake with a thick, soft cushion of grass for me to sit on. For Henry, the thinking tree served as an anchor for him to ponder and to reconnect to the earth.

Discover your own thinking tree. Do you have a tree that's special to you? If not, find one. Find a quiet spot in the shade under a tree in your yard, near your job, or in a local park, that feels "right" to sit under and recharge.

Go to your tree and sit with your back against the tree. Take your shoes off, let your bare feet touch the earth. Sit quietly and observe what's happening around you.

- Close your eyes and listen to the sounds you hear.

- Feel the air, the sun. Is there a breeze? Can you feel the warmth of the sun on your skin?

- Where are you in your thinking—the past, present, or future? Bring your thoughts into the present.

Bring your attention to the tree and feel its wisdom connecting with your innate ability to connect with your soul's wisdom. Can you feel its energy boost as it connects with yours?

- Allow the tree's energy to help you find the answers to problems you wish to resolve. Let the tree lift the weight of those things from your spirit and send it up into the light.

• Allow yourself to relax and know that the answers you seek are available. As you tune inward, you will know what it is that you need to know, what actions to take, and what to do next.

Practice this often to get in the habit of tuning in and recharging. Afterward, journal the messages that come through your meditations under your own thinking tree.

chapter 5
Weight as a Mask

As I am rushing to get downstairs to greet my next client, I see a gentleman sitting alone in the upstairs waiting area at the center. I stop and introduce myself, asking if he is by chance waiting for me. He is and introduces himself as George. I am immediately drawn in by his captivating dark eyes that smile when he talks. George is here to explore issues with being severely overweight and overeating that have plagued him most of his life.

As I walk with him back to my office, he tells me that he is curious to explore whether his weight issues in his current life have to do with "carry over" from a previous one. He already knows of one past life in which he describes himself as being a "skinny hunter" whose brother, the strong, muscular tribal leader, got all the attention. He is curious to know if there are more.

George begins to tell me about his current life history regarding weight. When he was very young, his mother died. He was adopted and raised as an only child after being separated from his younger siblings. Childhood was mostly uneventful except that his new family moved around a bit due to his father's job. George remembers that when he was a young boy his adoptive parents put locks on the refrigerator to keep him out because of his overeating, but he didn't consider himself large. By high school, he was about twenty pounds overweight.

When it came time to choose a career, George decided on the military and did very well on his placement exams. He naturally excelled at math and was placed on a high-tech science track, which he gladly accepted. During this time, George developed a habit of eating junk food throughout the night to stay awake during the long nights of training. To manage his weight, he stayed on a regimented exercise program. However, over the course of his training, his weight gain began to spiral out of control. George was eventually discharged from military service before he could finish the program, for being overweight.

George was surprisingly happy to be discharged. He celebrated his freedom by eating whatever he wanted and giving up his regimented exercise routine. He found a career in the private sector using his military training and worked his way up, doing very well for himself. The habit of eating during the night to stay awake on the job continued and George's weight spiraled even further out of control. Late-night eating became the norm. By this point the weight created difficulty with mobility and balance. It inhibited his ability to walk up and down steps or to get up out of a chair easily.

So, we begin the All Lives Session and George moves to a pleasant time during his fifth birthday party. "Georgie" is wearing a cowboy hat and holding a big birthday cake in his lap while his adoptive father takes pictures of him with the other kids to celebrate the occasion. Next, George moves back in time to the womb where he feels his birth mother's heartbeat and hears the muffled sounds of those around her. This is another pleasant memory for him, so he spends some time here enjoying the comfort of his birth mother's heartbeat and the chance to reconnect with her before continuing.

George easily drifted from the womb experience and found his way along his soul's history to a lifetime that was relevant to his current life weight and overeating concerns. He landed in a scene on a battlefield in WWI wearing an American uniform and battle gear. He was a tall, lanky young man, only twenty-four years old, with blonde hair and blue eyes.

He could hear someone next to him address him as "sergeant" and felt himself trying to keep his helmet on his head as he turned toward that direction. He answered to the title of sergeant but gave his full name as Sergeant Harvey Wiseman. He observed the young recruit next to him—"the Kid," as he called Private Gorham—who stood dutifully awaiting instructions from the sergeant. The troops were preparing for the impending battle that was making its way toward them. He explained that as a leader it was his job to first and foremost keep the men in line, keep them ready, and keep morale up.

As the sergeant heard himself reply to the Kid, he noticed he spoke with a distinct accent, quickly realizing he was British. He clarified that he was an Englishman by birth, but he and his mother had come to the States before the war had begun. She found work in a laundry and Harvey had joined the army as a means of gaining American citizenship.

Harvey confided that although he had experience and training, most of the time he felt like he had no idea what he was doing. "Although you're never ready for the battle," he stated, "you just hope to God you survive it." He couldn't let his men know he felt this way, so he put on a brave face and did what he had to do. He found himself constantly giving his unit, especially the Kid, instructions and a pep talk. As the battle moved closer, mortar shells landed close enough that they could feel them. The sergeant bravely looked into the Kid's eyes and told him to put his heart into that gun and into serving his country. You don't know the outcome but need to put your heart into it as you see your way through it. This is what counts.

The fighting had reached the trenches where the sergeant and his men lay waiting. The sergeant's men proudly came up out of the trench, firing their weapons as mortar shells were coming down upon them. It was difficult to see through the haze it stirred up. "I just tell my men to keep moving, some get shot and killed ... but I have to keep them moving," the sergeant said. They fired in the direction of the enemy, not knowing if they hit anyone or not. At that moment, there was an explosion. The sergeant was hit first in his right leg by a bullet and was simultaneously knocked unconscious as he fell to the ground.

Waking up in the infirmary, the sergeant felt the pain of his bandaged leg and head as he saw the Kid standing by his bedside. The Kid was excited to be the one to tell the sergeant that "We did it, we pushed the enemy back."

So that was it for the sergeant and the war. He left when he was able to limp out of the infirmary with the aid of a cane. Harvey went back to the States and worked as an army recruiter after the war. As his leg began to heal, he was relieved that he no longer needed the cane to be able to walk. He decided to keep the cane though because it made a great story for recruiting.

Harvey spent the rest of his days as a recruiter and his nights at the local pub. He never started a family of his own. Instead he kept himself busy, surrounded by many friends so as not to feel alone or regretful looking back at what might have been. Harvey ate well and drank well, masking any feelings of regret with his great sense of humor and stories of the war. He was still tall but had put on weight and had a pot belly from developing what he called a case of "the creeps." "That's what they call it when it just creeps up on you," Harvey laughed.

Harvey's growing weight eventually led to a heart attack in his mid-fifties one evening while leaving the pub with his friends. As he lay dying, his last thoughts were of the advice he had given to the Kid years before, hoping that the young recruit had followed that advice and kept his own heart in the right place.

Harvey's guide greets him as he crosses into the spirit world. After a brief time in a place of rest and rejuvenation, he is taken to a room that is similar to a movie viewing room with a small screen and projector for Soul Reflection. Here he discovers that the purpose of that life had been leadership. He is told that as with everything, there is a spectrum to leadership. With leadership you have the people at the top controlling and leading the great numbers, while others participate at the bottom leading those around them. Harvey's role was to lead those at the bottom.

His guide further explains that this went back to the pep talk there in the trenches with the Kid where he had advised him, "Don't worry about what happens to you as long as you put your heart into what you do. Where you put your heart is what matters." Harvey used that a lot in life whether going into battle or with recruiting new recruits.

So here we are with a really great session, but we still don't know what this has to do with George's current life concerns about his weight or overeating, which was the reason for the session. And here is another lifetime of food and drink, this time to mask feelings of loneliness and regret. Coincidentally, in his current life George has also been in the US military, but had gotten out just after getting in, so we ask for help from his spiritual team to help us to understand the current life parallels to these two issues here.

First, George is told that the significance in choosing a life as a soldier was to awaken the understanding within him that when it comes to leading, it isn't always about being in front for everyone to follow. Leadership is about being in the midst of it all and nudging in the right direction. George can lead by gently nudging others like the Kid, who in his current life continues to look up to him, the way he had when George was the sergeant. He can also learn to make better choices with food and drink than the sergeant had made and finally break the habit of late night eating he developed.

Second, his guide explains the significance of George having also been in the military in his current life: it was just enough to get George moving to where he needed to be going. His spiritual team advises him that he was never supposed to finish the science program; he was just supposed to start it. What may have appeared to be a "poor choice" in starting something he didn't finish was actually needed to guide George in the right direction.

Lastly, George is told that the lifetime as the sergeant held the key to the message that he holds inside himself that he needed to hear again. Those words he gave as a battlefield pep talk for the Kid that also served him during the remainder of his own life as the sergeant, are the same words that George needs now to wake him up in his current situation.

His guide then clarifies that George is to remember the message in his current life, that it's not about going through the motions, but putting his heart into things that he does. No more procrastinating—he's to get started on his true passion, which is writing. George is told not to worry about being great, or how it will all turn out, just to put his heart into his well-thought-out-stories and get them out of his head and onto paper. The unfinished stories and looking back to what might have been are what have been "weighing on him." George is reminded that his energy and his body are both interconnected. He is assured that following his passion for writing will free up his energy and allow him to lose the weight.

There is a lesson here about learning to appreciate choices that get you to your present situation and in moving on without regret or looking back to what might have been. These choices are meant to get you to where you are now.

Before the close of the session, George is given a symbol to remember the session by, which he recognizes as something he often doodles when contemplating a story idea. He immediately feels lighter, as if a burden has been lifted, and he is more focused on what it is that he needs to do next. No more procrastinating or staying stuck; it's time to move forward in life with his writing instead.

Since the time of his session, George is now following his passion and his heart, putting both into his stories, which have been well received by his readers. George is learning to appreciate all of the choices, good and bad, that have led him to where he is now. He understands the deeper meaning, that following his heart is his connection to his soul, and he recognizes the many great stories his choices have given him to write about.

—— *Soul-Minded Journaling* ——
What Is Your Weight Masking?

What are you "weighting" for in your own life? What emotions are weighing you down? What areas of your life are you procrastinating about? What regrets have you looking back at what could have been? Is there a situation from your past that you need to make peace with? Are you just going through the motions in life? What are you passionate about? What's your heart's desire?

Are you using food and drink as a mask to avoid dealing with those emotions or to avoid taking steps toward your goals in life? Do you feel that you have to be "out in front," making big gestures in order to help others or achieve your goals, or can you make desired changes without it being disruptive and needlessly turning your life upside down?

Look for ways to achieve your goals more smoothly and easily, beginning with where you are right now in your life and taking small, steady steps toward them. Are you so focused on the outcome that you can't seem to get started in the present? What is holding you back? What are you waiting for?

What does your future hold? Sit with your feelings. Where is your heart?

What would you like to create in your life if you could have your "heart's desire"?

Entertain those thoughts of what it would look like and feel like to have your heart's desire fulfilled. Feel it and really own it as you do!

Now write a short, empowering statement that strengthens you and moves you toward this goal as you repeat it to yourself. (Ex. Every day I am taking steps to be free of the excess weight.

Every day I am happy and healthy in my thoughts and choices. I appreciate my past and my choices for what it has taught me and for bringing me to this present moment in my life.)

Put it on a sticky note in a place that you'll see it throughout your day (refrigerator, computer, car).

Repeat your empowering statement ten times each morning when you wake up, throughout your day, and ten times at night just before bed. Put your heart into it and feel it as you do this.

chapter 6
Authenticity and Breaking Negative Money Patterns

Linda comes for a SESR session, gifted to her by a friend, to help her find deeper understanding regarding issues with poverty consciousness. She admits feeling overwhelmed and weighed down, as if she'll never get ahead. She is trying to get back on her feet after her divorce, despite her ex-husband's attempts to use money to sabotage or exert control over her.

She confesses that money has always been a sticking point in their relationship. Linda tells me that years ago she left her career to stay home with their young children at his encouragement, but soon realized she had lost the ability to make choices with how they spent their money. Despite having a good job, it seemed as if the more money he had, the more he spent on expensive electronic gadgets and toys, instead of necessities for the kids.

She believes him to be angry at her for leaving him, so instead of paying child-support payments to Linda to take care of their children, he gives the money directly to the kids and tells them to just buy whatever they need with it. This puts Linda in the unpleasant position of having to ask her teenage children for money to pay the electric bill or buy groceries. It isn't fair to put the children in the middle this way and it leaves her financially unstable because she can't use it where it's needed. Without money, she can't hire an attorney to fight for her either.

Linda does what she can but her modest job as a medical receptionist isn't enough to cover expenses. It provides some comfort knowing she at least has medical care for her kids and a consistent schedule, but the meager salary leaves her feeling defenseless and her cupboards are bare. At one point, things get so bad she finds herself facing eviction.

So, we begin Linda's session to seek answers to why she's faced the financial struggles she has. She popped into a past life scene in the mid-1700s, in which she was stooped over weeding the flowerbeds in front of her home dressed in traditional Dutch clothing—wooden shoes and a hand-sewn, apron-like dress with a white cap. She was thirteen years old and had outgrown this style many years before, but her parents insisted she still wear the "costume."

Helene, an only child, lived with her parents in a modest home in the small village of Schwevingnennen, near Den Haag where wealthy tourists vacationed by the North Sea. Her mother made cakes that she sold in town and her father did odd jobs around town.

They were a family of pretense, but not in the normal sense. They dressed in dowdy handmade costumes, pretending to be poor so that the tourists strolling by would take pity and "throw coin" at their young daughter, Helene, who was instructed to weed the flowerbeds, making sure to be seen by the passersby. Helene never picked up the coins, but rather her parents gathered them up frequently, so it didn't appear they had collected much. To keep up their beggarly image, her parents refused to be seen owning nice things. They bartered in town for chickens and milk because it was too risky to be seen with a cow; only the more well-off families could afford one.

Helene's father went so far as to build a secret room inside their house that was kept hidden from everyone, including the neighbors and friends. Her mother called this her "room of belongings" where they kept their most precious things. Her mother liked beautiful lace and fabric, but it could never be enjoyed publicly because she wouldn't allow people to see that they lived a comfortable life.

Helene described her life as being an "artificial life" because no one in her house was allowed to be authentic. Her parents believed they had to hide who they were in order to get by. Helene always obeyed her parents and did as was expected, so hiding her wealth and her identity became a way of life for young Helene too. During this era, only priests and a few males were formally taught to read; however, Helene's father had been educated in secret. Because he had no son to pass this down to, he taught Helene, who eagerly learned to read, reason, and converse—another secret to keep.

As time went on, Helene grew into a beautiful young woman. A young man named Peter was attracted to Helene on a visit to the village and asked her father for her hand in marriage. Peter was from a wealthy family who made their fortune dealing in rugs and tapestries. He and his family were influential members of a merchants' guild that could manipulate governments and the church behind the scenes to give them a monopoly on the market.

Peter was a great negotiator and skilled at manipulating almost any situation to get what he wanted. In this case, he wanted Helene. Helene's father agreed to the marriage, only after Peter promised to take care of her parents in return. Peter only saw beauty when he looked at Helene. He liked her smile and her laugh. He believed she'd be a healthy wife and give him many children. Helene did not want to marry Peter or have children, but she did as she was told.

Helene moved to Delft to Peter's beautifully appointed home. Peter loved her and wanted her to have the very best of things. There were always servants afoot who took care of everything. Helene happily accepted their help with women's household matters which she had no interest in.

Their relationship was somewhat odd. The conversations over the years with her own father about business, travel, and tourism had given Helene the ability to converse with Peter on business, offering advice and suggestion. She enjoyed this, aware that most women of the day did not and could not do this. They weren't allowed to read or write, much less reason.

Although Helene tried to be a good wife and give Peter children, none of the children she bore survived beyond birth. Helene believed it to be her punishment for not loving Peter as much as he loved her, so she spent time in church repenting for her sins. Not long after the death of their youngest infant, Helene agreed to allow Peter's illegitimate son and his mistress, Elisabeth, to move into their home in Delft so Peter could give the child his blessing and acknowledge the child as his own. It was Helene who suggested that Elisabeth move in too.

It was an extremely emotional time for Helene following the loss of her youngest child, but she gratefully welcomed Elisabeth and the child into her home. In contrast to Helene, who was now older, Elisabeth was young and beautiful, and they lived in a society that openly acknowledged liaisons of this type. This was the opposite of the pretense Helene was forced to endure while growing up. Helene didn't want the pressure of pretense or the responsibility of raising the boy as her own. Now she was off the hook, oddly free of the pressure to produce a son; and now that there was a mistress, oddly free to be left alone.

With more time available to her, Helen spent even more time in the Catholic Church, finding comfort there following the loss of her babies and of her husband's affections. She was tormented with guilt that she didn't return Peter's feelings to the same degree. He was a good man and she even felt betrayed by her own feelings toward him.

Despite the strange relationship between them, Helene continued the conversations with Peter about business and trade, but now only when she was asked. Other times she'd overhear Peter in his office having discussions with other businessmen involving the Templars' and the Masons' plans. These discussions were about secret plans to block merchant ships and share government information that wasn't meant to be publicly disclosed. She learned in advance of visits from high ranking government officials, foreign dignitaries, and other prominent members of her husband's social circle.

The Dutch masters were powerful and had commerce and money to lend at a time where there was chaos and war in France. The French and English hated one another and the new country, the New Americas, only added more fuel to the fire by trying to establish their freedom from England. At this time no one liked the English—their politics, their control, or their taxation.

There had to be a break from the corruption that existed. The American rebellion that was brewing was a way to divide and conquer the fundamentalist groups that had initially been responsible for the New Americas. Europe was becoming too hedonistic and not reflecting good morals, but rather the "morals of the devil." Helene considered it her duty to help.

Helene started documenting what she heard, realizing she was positioned to assist. She felt compelled to act, almost not caring if she got caught. It was imperative to keep her country out of war.

Over time Helene took the information she collected, mostly banking and finance-related, to influential confidantes at her church to undermine the efforts of the guildsmen. It wasn't her intention to incriminate Peter or hurt him in any way. Her sole interest was in supporting the New World and saving her country from possible war and harm as a result of the impending American rebellion being orchestrated by these powerful groups.

Helene didn't always write the notes she delivered, but she found she could easily decipher the codes passed between the guild, Templars, and Masons to thwart their plans for the impending revolution. She acted as a go-between. She found it entertaining and invigorating, and she was a key figure, a double agent. Others in the network, Templars and Masons alike, were instructed to bring her notes, often in symbol form or a secret language designed to confuse, which she'd either read to them or pass on to others through the confessionals at church. In later years, Helene traveled to Belgium and other cathedrals, leaving pieces of paper with notes and symbols behind related to the government, the guild, and the church.

During this time, if someone had something to be read, they were to take it to a priest who would read it for them. So, the guildsmen were not aware where this information was being leaked. Helene could read, write, and reason, so many a note was passed off as a grocery list. She did it covertly and carefully, no one suspecting a thing, certainly not from a woman.

Dressed in beautiful, luxurious outfits signifying a woman of wealth, Helene walked quietly by open doors or through church corridors unnoticed. From the days of her childhood forced to wear costumes and those horrible wooden shoes, she now detested wearing shoes at all. She'd wear shoes in public, but around her home she enjoyed the freedom of walking barefoot through the halls where she could quietly pass by and listen through cracked doorways virtually unheard. And it was having grown up living a double life that made this come so easily to Helene.

As the years passed, Peter and Helene began to lead separate lives. He had his with his family and hers now had purpose. Helene continued to accompany Peter to certain social events or entertain important guests in their home. In town they were a well-respected family, yet both Helene and Peter were secretly and separately running an underground railroad. She often put him in danger in his own home. They would entertain but Peter would have no idea who some of these individuals were, sometimes hosting dissidents passing through from Germany or Rome to cross to major port cities, taking messages with them across the channel.

Helene was respected in her own right. Men in her husband's social circle saw Helene as a good wife for allowing her husband's illegitimate child and his mistress into her home.

They often turned to her for help with alternative family planning such as this for their own families.

Helene contributed where she could. The information she passed, more financially-related than anything, was designed to support the New Americas. She provided Thomas Jefferson with information because it was important he get support from the Dutch bankers, but admitted that she didn't like or trust Ben Franklin because of his loyalty to the English. She didn't meet with Jefferson directly. Instead she passed papers containing secret notes via courier.

At this time, not much was known about this new country. America wasn't like other countries in Europe where one could travel from one border to the next. It was, instead, a dangerous journey, not a casual touring as one was accustomed to in Europe. Information then had to be deciphered once it was delivered.

Helene got away with passing secrets for this and other causes she was passionate about for many, many years. She was caught several times. Protected by her family's prominent name and the belief that, being an old woman, she couldn't really comprehend the true nature of the information she passed along or the seriousness of what she had done, Helene was gently reprimanded and then released. She lived out the remainder of her life quiet, but proud of her efforts.

As Helene leaves that life, crossing into the spirit world she is lovingly greeted by her guide. She's happy to see him. He showers her with an energy of renewal that lifts the residue of that life from her spirit.

In Soul Reflection her guide shares with her more about that life and its connection to others who incarnate when a shift is needed on Earth. He explains that "souls incarnated into places designed to help the world evolve this way as part of a larger plan for the government of the New Americas to be established ... these highly evolved souls are strategically placed in order to facilitate their soul's evolution and for the good of the Earth by going above and beyond ego, control, and human characteristics ... "

Linda's guide speaks of a Brotherhood/Sisterhood of Light that goes beyond those on Earth. He explains that other groups are about fear, control, and secrecy, where the Brotherhood/Sisterhood of the Light is about assistance, empowerment, and allowance. Countless highly advanced souls, both male and female, went about their work unnoticed by society but played key roles in its advancement, and the shift was created in the world as the creation of the New Americas came about. At a soul level, they had a choice of whether to incarnate into a human body or to assist on the other side of the veil.

Souls bring their talents and skills to the table. They are strategically placed in terms of geography, relationships, and birth years, and are part of a divine plan for guidance to help Earth move along ... each entity has a divine purpose, each one is special and unique, yet there would be nothing but chaos without order. It is a human concept that someone must know more to be better. The divine plan is about order ... everyone brings their skills to the table to create it.

He reveals, "It is an influx of need and desire with a consciousness shift now for so many to currently be on this Earth to incarnate as a group of strategically placed entities involved in some way with communication, interpretation, intuition, and processing information—whether symbol, song, prayer, pose or any type of information—gathering as well as relaying information where it is needed."

Her guide explains that those that bring the light are not concerned with control. Others undermine the progression of the Earth by their control and negativity. They take the knowledge that is meant to be available to all and control it. That is not the original intention of the information. It is often lower-level souls who do this because lower-level souls are drawn to fear and control. Do not give them energy. He advises that when light shines on darkness, it eradicates darkness and truth is revealed.

The mission of the Brotherhood/Sisterhood is to be beacons of hope, faith, and guidance to all who choose to look at the light. It is about courage and determination of souls who know purpose and do not falter in moving forward.

He explains that having your own purpose and following your heart and joy put you where you need to be to transmit information from one beacon to another as souls. It keeps souls aligned with the planetary energy grids and keeps the energy flowing for the human experience, otherwise lessons cannot take place. There are many levels of souls and many job descriptions in the spirit world.

Linda's soul carries a gentler energy than that of her guide. In Soul Awareness she begins speaking directly, revealing that her spiritual team had arranged for Linda to have a SESR session because "we believed it was time for her to understand her purpose." Her soul reveals, "Her current incarnation is exactly as planned. Nothing has been altered; it is for Linda to be content and accepting as she has begun to come to terms and be at peace with being on her own...."

Next Linda's guide shows her ways she can align with more joy in her life and utilize her own gifts to move into her new career. She recognizes how fear and worry result in extra weight—

physically and emotionally—while joy lightens. He also helps to resolve some of the conflicting beliefs she held regarding money. He explains that money is not to be held on to tightly, feared, or blocked. Money is a currency that must flow.

In her current life Linda was at the mercy of her children for money, just as in the past life Helene was dependent on her parents for money. Soul Recognition revealed the connection to some of the people from the past life to Linda's life today. There are patterns to be broken and lessons for them all.

Linda has grown through conflicts with relationships of the heart and conflicts of ethics. Helene lived a life of pretense as a child and then again as an adult. She learned to live a double life—giving an outward appearance as one thing and inwardly doing another. In her current incarnation, Linda couldn't pretend anymore. Pretending in her marriage was killing her inside and, in turn, setting a bad example for her children. It was killing her to not be able to be who she was or to be authentic, so she did what she had to do to get out of the situation.

This difficult period in Linda's life has helped her to find inner strength she didn't know that she had, during a time of true crisis. It also taught her the value in giving her children her attention, which at the time was about all she had left to give. Spending time with them in conversation about the events of their day helped them all through the crisis and into healing. It helped them find strength too. Leaving the comfort of their materially-rich home for one that was spiritually rich but materially bare during the years of that transition after the divorce had taught them about money.

Revisiting this past life is helping Linda to break the long-standing pattern of poverty consciousness. She's able to see herself differently and because of this she can shift into a healthier relationship with herself. She understands why she has a driving urge to live a life of authenticity and to not pretend that something is other than what it actually is.

As Linda has begun to value herself, she's attracting others into her life that do, too. She has a new job with lots of supporters who value her for who she is. Even the relationship with her ex-husband is improving. Linda is happy with herself and the new life she is building.

—— *Soul-Minded Journaling* ——
Shifting Your Relationship with Money

Where is your outward appearance at odds with your inner self? Are you being authentic or are you too caught up in having more stuff?

What is your relationship to money? Do you see money as a flow of energy, currency helping you to get where you need to be in life, or do you see money as a struggle, something hard to hold on to or have enough of? Are you spending money unnecessarily in any areas of your life? Are there things you're holding on to that could bring you freedom and money by letting them go? Do you believe there's enough money for you to have your share or do you believe there's never enough?

Observe your thoughts and feelings about money and having things. What beliefs do you have about money? Write them down in your journal.

Do those things have you feeling tied down, or do you feel joyful when you look around you at what you have? Look around your home. What do the things around you say about you? Do you like them or feel stuck by them? Are there things you could sell to make room for things you'd enjoy?

What are some healthier attitudes you would like to cultivate regarding money?

On another note, what is something you've always wanted that you've never allowed yourself to have? Would it enhance your life or cause things to be out of balance? Start small. Choose something relatively inexpensive that you've denied yourself from having that would give you great joy, like a piece of clothing, crafts, a hobby, a nice dinner out, or a drive to a beautiful place near where you live. It doesn't have to be expensive; this is meant to start a flow of money in your life. Don't break the budget to do it. If you need to, save up for it. You'll appreciate it even more once you allow yourself to have it, or you may decide once you can afford it, it's not important to you after all.

Start small, allowing yourself to have things you like. Perhaps get a money tree or aloe vera plant for your home or office to set the intention for new streams of money to come into your life or for healing financial issues of the past. Remember to water it and repeat your intention to yourself frequently to strengthen the flow of new money coming your way.

chapter 7
The Gifts You
Brought with You

Claire is interested in a SESR to explore and recharge. "I want to be aware of the afterlife in this plane, hold a little piece of it in my heart and let it recharge me," she shared. What follows reveals that all lives have meaning. If you think your life is insignificant or has no meaning, you are incorrect. Your existence affects others one way or the other simply by your having been here. There's an energetic exchange upon remembrance by the parties involved.

The SESR session begins. Floating along the current of her soul's consciousness, Claire ends up in the womb where she experiences a bit of her mother's distress. She can feel her mother's energy shooting through her tiny body at this midway point between the seventh and eighth month of development. It is close to the time when she is to be born. It is becoming more difficult for her mother, who is nervous and stressed about having another child so quickly after their first one. Claire's father feels distant to Claire, as if he looks at having children as just something that people are expected to do.

Her mother is not pleased with the pregnancy part of motherhood and wants to get this part over with as quickly as possible. During this developmental period when Claire can "feel" her mother's stress levels surge, she tries to remain calm and send that calmness back to her mother. Claire is glad and excited to be born, constantly thanking her for agreeing to be her mother this time around.

Claire's spirits are high. She knows she is coming to bring enthusiasm and spread it around. It's needed on Earth and she happily signed up for it. She will do this in many ways through what she does, and when she writes. Claire has boundless energy and is bringing it to Earth to share. She too shares her mother's feelings of wanting to get through the pregnancy period and get on with being born.

Since the fifth month, Claire's spirit has stayed in the body to get aligned with it, rather than traveling back "home" to prepare. Much of her time is spent floating and sleeping, planning and observing her thoughts about what she'll need for the life that is coming.

Suspended there, she receives information that flows directly into her cells. These instructions are sent from "home"— from that place where they help you build your "suit with your traits that you're going to be," Claire explains. You start out with what you come in with and can change how you see and move around in the world. These instructions are stored and remembered later when you need them.

These downloads contain information about the person that she will be. She reveals that the soul helps create the part of the suit where you agree what you'll be. Then the ones who help you in prebirth planning tell you how that will happen and the traits and personality that go with that. It's talked about, planned, and designed by them for you before you incarnate. They're like tailors. They take what you're planning to come for and make a suit for you to wear.

I ask Claire to tell me more about her prebirth planning. She clarifies that she knew she would be incarnating and would need a lot of enthusiasm, energy, the sense of that "I can do it!" feeling with her this time. Her soul works with her spiritual team of guides and her Soul Advisory Council in prebirth planning to give her what she will need for this incarnation as Claire. They give you the pieces you'll need to remember to do when you incarnate. The suit has the memories in it, so they activate later when you need them.

I probe further, asking how this body will help her with what she is coming to do. "You can't see the suit," she explains. "At different times it will help you to do what you're supposed to do, like how you see the world... it's on the inside. It's what makes you laugh at some things and not others. It's hooked in. It's the suit you put on to get born and has all you need in it. You hook into what you'll need while you're here, like how you see different than someone else does, it's all there... it's your 'Birthday Suit.'"

The amount of energy a soul brings in for an incarnation varies depending on what's required for the lifetime. Some souls bring more, others bring less. Claire knew she would need more energy this time because she has a big job to do, so she brought about 70 percent more this time, knowing there are a lot of unhappy people whom she has agreed to help.

Claire notices a door she is meant to go through. She knows she can enter it just by looking at it. She glances at it and slips inside. On the other side of the doorway are stars everywhere. She goes directly into the cosmic realms, bypassing a past life. It feels light, free, and quiet to be there. Suddenly a ball of light appears. It is her guide, whom she is meant to follow. He patiently takes her slowly along this pathway through the stars, so she can feel them and absorb the atmosphere here.

Next, Claire is taken to a place where other spirits are around her. She's curious to see her soul group, the group of souls who incarnate together, playing different roles in one another's lives throughout their various incarnations. They take on roles to help each other learn and experience. Claire's guide tells her it isn't time yet. She passes several family members she recognizes from her current life, some living and some deceased, who smile at her as she passes by. Because a part of one's soul remains in the spirit world while one incarnates, souls are able to be in the spirit world in session and also in her current life as people Claire knows.

They continue to the Soul Awareness Area. Here Claire is shown pieces of everything. All kinds of things she has done are playing on a big viewing screen. There are also images she doesn't recognize. These are places and people that she is instructed are important to see in case she might need them.

Along with the images, Claire receives a lot of information through an energy download that makes her feel tingly as it activates a soul recalibration. As I sit and observe, I am reminded that Earth is an emotional planet. It's the planet where souls come to experience the range of emotions. All emotions are here. Half the battle of existing on this planet is managing one's emotions. Some get here and tend to get stuck in either the good or the bad, forgetting they can move through the emotions and don't have to limit themselves or their perception to just one.

Next, Claire is joined by the others who tell her there is more work to do. Emotional help is needed on Earth and that is the team she is on. "There are many changes coming our way on Earth. They 'think' it into your head. I'm to help with compassion. It's what's needed to help with these changes. The pulse of Earth is changing, it's beating faster, and some can't take the shift," she reveals. "The vibration is changing because it's not good how it is now. Lots of different people will soon be helping…teams of them…the pulse of all the spirits are all changing. We will be different, we'll change with it."

Claire is shown a heartbeat that speeds up and slows down. A piece is placed in her heart to hold as a reminder. It feels like blood pulsing through her veins. She understands this pulsing is happening around the planet, explaining that where souls meet is in that changed vibration. Claire knows instinctively that the energy of the heartbeat is shifting her into the right vibration for the work she is to do.

After a while, Claire's guide instructs her to follow him to another space, where she's surrounded by lights of different colors and begins to feel a pressure on the crown of her head. She reveals that this is a space for creating. Here, souls talk about things and then create them. She explains this is a place where you can "see" what you "think." What you think you can then create.

The creative space opens up to a big field, which she tells me is a metaphor for one's energy field. Her guide tells her you can think anything. He shows her that she can do that and always could. What's held her back was not believing that she can.

The space starts to clear out as souls begin leaving. It is busy with souls moving about and going places. She asks about her soul group again and this time they appear. As a group, their common goal is to bring love and happiness down to Earth. They all do this differently, with the ultimate goal being to bring the vibration up by allowing happiness and joy. There is a lot of love in Claire's soul group.

One group member brings back love from her travels and "puts" it into the energy field of others, so they can feel it too. Another, a driver for a ride-sharing service in a scenic part of the country, has a special connection to Earth. He pulls this energy in for his passengers to connect to along scenic routes on the way to their destination. Another member of the group works with geometry. Math, lines, and grids are the tools he uses to create spaces that people connect through. And lastly, the final member of the group helps bring order to those around him.

As they finish up here, Claire's guide instructs her it is time to go back to the Soul Awareness area. He senses a bit of apprehension from her and tells her not to be afraid, that all the information is there so she'd understand it.

It is vast and beautiful here and holds the knowledge about all souls. Claire explains to me that "everything is here and there is information everywhere—who you are and who you always were...not just you but everyone you know, so much, I'm in awe...it's all here, backward and forward from all of your lifetimes." Claire feels more energy downloading as a continuation of her soul recalibration. She is reminded of her soul name, which means "to give." As a soul she is a peacemaker and brings the desire to give and to pass love into each of the lifetimes she lives.

In Soul Reflection, she recalls a past life where she had not spoken up for someone and it cost them their life. Following a scuffle in a marketplace, the man she loved was falsely accused of stealing. Ali was her name then. A young Arab woman of about twenty years old, she had been afraid to get involved and afraid they wouldn't believe her if she stepped up because she was a woman. She watched as they hauled him away in an open cart. He looked to her, pleading with his dark eyes for her help. She hid under her hooded veil, ashamed of herself for pretending not to know him.

She lost her life too when she lost her love. She punished herself for not speaking out on his behalf by living out her days in a cave. Lonely and isolated, she died looking much older than her years from living with the sadness and despair in the aftermath of her selfishness and what she had done.

Her guide does not scold her as she had initially feared; he only shows her what transpired. She is shown that he might have had a chance had she spoken up, but she didn't even try. It may not have ended better for him, but even if she hadn't been able to stop it, she would have been able to live with herself knowing that she had tried.

In her current life, she has the opportunity to overcome this karmic carryover. Her guide tells her to find her voice now, to believe in herself. He shows her a pattern set by people in her life who have taught her by their example to hold back and not stand out. He explains how everyone has a role and plays a part. Claire is shown how she's learned this behavior and how she's held herself back by not speaking up more or sooner. He gives her a sword of light to use when she needs to speak up, so she won't be afraid to use her voice. He also tells her not to be so hard on herself as he reminds her that she is learning and can speak up without giving her power away. She's learning to use her art and her writing to express herself too.

The energy of compassion is palpable in the room as the soul of Ali's lost love shows up in her soul group and lets her know that all is forgiven. He had signed up for it and knew going in that he was going to die no matter what.

They continue on with an overview of lifetimes, so she can see how sometimes it is good and sometimes not good. Her soul reveals that this current time is important. She is not to give up, she is to keep going. There is light and there is resistance, but it can all be overcome. She's to remember what she came in with and use that. Everything has been leading up to this one. All of it!

Assurances are made that all of the people on her team have incarnated this time. No one is missing; not even Ali's lost love. She's told to trust this last part that her group will be doing together. She is given glimpses of world events where everything is shifting. Some people feel despair. Claire knows despair and can help them with that.

Her guide shows a vase falling with a crack in the inner piece [peace]. This was a metaphor for watching the thoughts and the big confusion that is occurring with humans. He shares: "Lightworkers and others are fixing it. World events are happening so people are confused, scared, and acting out in dark ways. We're not to be without hope, we can fix it... show different hands reaching up doing this work in many ways. The act of everyone working to soften the changes is part of their global purpose. We don't have to be fearful; there's a much bigger plan."

Shifts in financial markets in the United States in past years have caused people to scramble and be confused. More will occur, but assurances were given that a whole new way is coming. Initially, people will be confused and won't know what to think. They're to know that they've outgrown the way the current financial system is run. These changes have to happen to make way for a new thought.

As the financial system changes, negativity will go with it. There will be a new type of exchange. People will understand about helping people. They won't have things to hold over one another and will help each other out instead. It will be natural to help one another. That concept is far away from where things are right now. Souls and spirits on all dimensions are assisting with this shift. Not to worry, this shift will be like a "reset" that returns people to a simpler way.

Souls signed on to be here for this time in history. It will all be fine. Changes will come out for the better. Signals from our spiritual teams will come to guide those who pay attention to make the changes as needed, so they can do the work they came to do. Compassion will be a big part of it. You can't put a price on enthusiasm. It will be a valued commodity in the future during these shifts.

Her guide signals it is time for Claire to visit with her Soul Advisory Council. The Soul Advisory Council goes by many names—Elders, Wise Beings, the Wise Ones. They are a group of wise beings, like a special committee, that supports souls with all phases of their incarnations. Claire is led into a big, big, big room where five white light beings are waiting. She feels nervous to be in their presence. Her guide is there with her, reminding her this is a safe place. Her Elders make her feel comfortable and she stops feeling as if she is being judged by them when she realizes she was judging herself. They smile and tell her they are pleased with her and how she's behaved. Now, she's to finish what she incarnated for. This is not a time to be passive, it's a time to step up. She's reminded to hold love and compassion and to take in everyone that needs it.

The Elders let Claire know that they hear her when she asks for help and are giving her what she needs. The Elder on the left appears more lighthearted and the one on right is more serious, while the ones in the middle seemed to strike a balance. She tells me they've been with her for lifetimes and are with her now.

She is reminded of her first incarnation on Earth during the time of Jesus, but she was not part of Jesus's story. She lived in the same part of the world and everyone knew about him, but she never got to see him. In that life she was a stable boy. It was a lowly job, but she wasn't unhappy. That life was a re-minder about being humble, understanding, and making your own way. It didn't matter what your walk in life was, it was a chance to hold your head up no matter who you were or what you did. She did it with determination and this is being called for again now. No matter what you do you can make the best of it. Claire reminisces with her Soul Advisory Council about incarnations on other worlds and the struggles that went on.

The lighthearted Elder signals to Claire that it's time for her to come back. He laughs, divulging that the reason her Elders are all white light beings is to serve as a white light recharger for her spirit. "Recharge, recharge," he muses. "Go back, bring change, and be brave!" Her guide tells her to stop worrying so much about what she can see and not see. She carries the infor-mation in her "birthday suit" so she need not worry; she was born with everything she needs!

The session ends with a vision of many hands, those of people and other beings, working on the situation at hand. It's inevitable the vase will hit the ground, but it will be better after it does.

Following the session, Claire's energy seems stronger, with less worry and self-doubt. Clearing the past life energy through insightful review with her guide clears away insecurities and guilt she felt from it, and her energy field looks bright. She finds solace in knowing her connection to the divine.

Her sense of purpose is strengthened now that she has a clearer understanding of her uniqueness as a soul and as the person she is now. She finds comfort in knowing it is okay to speak up more and use her voice, and in knowing that she was born with everything she needs. She looks great and feels grateful to be charged up!

—— *Soul-Minded Journaling* ——
Recognizing Your Unique Gifts, Skills, and Abilities

Everyone has gifts or talents that make them unique. Sometimes people don't recognize their gifts as special, or they take them for granted, thinking everyone can do what they're able to do naturally. Use this journaling exercise to discover and identify your own gifts and abilities. Take time to really look at yourself objectively to uncover the qualities you possess.

• One way to recognize your gifts is to look back to your childhood. What kinds of things did you enjoy doing without being told to do them? What activities were you naturally good at in school or in your social life? Were you afraid or curious as a child? Were you outgoing or were you shy?

- What gifts, skills, and abilities do you possess in your current life? Do you recognize the gifts that make you special? Learn to recognize what's unique to you that you bring with you wherever you go. Do people turn to you for leadership, or a sense of comfort, or for a laugh because of your unique perspective on things? Do you have an upbeat attitude or sense of adventure? Are you a good listener or naturally organized? Do your talents lie in gardening or are animals naturally drawn to you? Are you good at building things or better at demolition? Are you great at manifesting things?

- What skills and abilities do you admire in others? What do others tell you they admire in you? Identify the special gifts you bring to your relationships and interactions with others.

- What are you naturally good at? What ways can you improve on strengths you naturally have, or overcome areas where you are deficient? What would you like to improve on? What abilities have you cultivated in yourself that you once admired in others? How do you feel about your abilities? How do they help you manage your life? Are you comfortable expressing who you are? What experiences or situations are keeping you from feeling comfortable being your true self? What makes you happy?

- Is your energy open and inviting, or restrictive and closed off? Find ways to boost your "birthday suit" to make your energy field fresh and new again! What makes you light up? What brings you joy?

chapter 8

Indecision and Self-Trust

I worked with Faith a few years back to resolve relationship issues. She's returned for a SESR session to figure out the next steps in her life. Her children are grown and have children of their own. While being a grandmother is fun, Faith has personal goals she wants to complete too. She seeks guidance as to which of three projects she should pursue, if any, and the courage to trust her intuition as she does.

The first project she considers is writing a book to leave behind for her children and grandchildren; the book will be about the interesting, undeniable synchronicities she has experienced during her life. She has traveled and lived all over the world to wherever her ex-husband's career took them. Her career has always been secondary to raising the children, but she has managed to get her degree and become a counselor out of the desire to help others. She feels compelled to write about her adventures and how her intuition and synchronicities have saved her from perilous situations more than a few times.

Faith has very strong intuitive skills, which she has repressed her entire life out of fear of being judged by others. As a teenager she had an interest in metaphysics and was even accepted to a parapsychology program at a prominent university well known for its metaphysical research; her parents preferred she choose a more traditional career path.

Faith was torn about which school to choose. She struggled with the decision, but her lack of courage caused her to change her plans and choose a traditional women's college instead. She grew up in a small town in the 1940s and '50s, and the world was a different place than it is now. She didn't like standing out from the crowd, so she kept her abilities to herself. Even as an adult she continues to keep her intuitive gifts a secret because the one or two times she has confided in a close friend, she felt their surprise and then concern.

The other two projects Faith has in mind are to either build a home on a piece of land she owns, or purchase a smaller, existing home to remodel. Faith and her ex-husband have lived in many homes in amazing places around the world and she enjoys remodeling them. She proudly shares with me that she has remodeled nearly thirty homes in her life and feels that she has one more remodel to do before she feels complete. While remodeling an existing home is not exciting, she considers it to be less of an undertaking than building from the ground up.

With all of these projects, Faith's intention is to leave something behind for her children. She believes her family might find the stories of her adventures interesting, while the properties could be something of monetary value they can benefit from too. Faith is at odds with what to do with the time she has left in her current life and wants clarity.

We begin the session with Faith moving through current life memories and into a corridor of light. It was gray and foggy. Immediately, she was shown a carved wooden chair sitting on a platform surrounded by tall pine trees. As she walked around the front of the chair, she saw herself wearing a long black skirt that fell to her ankles and her long gray hair spilling down her back. She was an old woman with a wrinkled face and graying eyes. She was aware this was a small hamlet in Germany during ancient times.

She saw herself standing over a man she held captive, holding an axe in her hands. He was dressed in peasant's clothing, with his hands tied behind his back. Her prisoner knelt before her with his head bowed. An angry crowd of onlookers watched intently. She knew they expected her to use the axe to behead her prisoner, yet she didn't want to do it. Facing a dilemma as to what to do next, she walked slowly, stalling for time, hoping someone else would step forward and offer to do it instead, but they did not.

The angry mob feared her for her powers as a witch but appreciated her healing abilities when people fell ill. She was torn as the wisdom of her years told her not to do this; she shouldn't kill this man no matter how much the crowd pressured her to. They had a right to be angry. He had stolen a baby and been found out. Although the child had been well cared for and they had gotten her back unharmed, the people still demanded he pay for his crime with his life. They didn't care that he had stolen the baby for his wife who was wrought with grief after their own tiny newborn, who had been weak, had died. She had asked him to find her a baby after she was told that she would never conceive again or be able to have children of her own.

The witch didn't believe this man would be a threat to anyone again. She could see he felt remorse for what he had done and she could see that the man's wife was beside herself. She had already lost her child and was about to lose her husband, too. The witch struggled with herself about what to do. What if she let him go and she was wrong?

Having finally made her decision, the witch knew what she had to do. She lifted the axe over her prisoner, bringing it down onto the ropes binding his hands to cut his hands free. He breathed a sigh of relief at being freed. The man and his wife were so grateful she had spared his life, and they promised not to steal any more children.

The crowd began to disperse but they were clearly not happy with her decision. They were angry at her for not chopping his head off then and there. Some wanted to chop her head off too. She told them she didn't believe the man would steal another child and if he did, it would be on her.

One man angrily pushed through the crowd toward her. It was the father of the child who had been taken. He picked up the axe and swung it at her, slicing her jugular vein as it cut into her neck. She lay on the ground weak and bleeding before she died there.

At the moment her spirit left her body, the witch could only think of how disappointed she was in the people. She was angry about being put in the position of having to decide another man's fate. She didn't want to be the one to make the decision. She just couldn't kill him. She understood why he took the child and she also realized why the child's father was understandably angry. Although the child had been returned to his parents unharmed, that wasn't enough for the outraged father. He wanted revenge. She considered for a moment what would happen to the angry father for killing her. Would he be killed for her murder? She felt sadness for his wife having to raise that baby alone. They would all pay the price for him losing his temper.

The first figure to greet her in the spirit world is dressed as a character out of a children's storybook. He is wearing a top hat and a long black coat. His face is covered with black whiskers and he holds a walking stick in his hand. He resembles a combination of Ichabod Crane from the headless horseman story; Abraham Lincoln; and a small business owner she knew in her current life. Faith comments that she feels a bit like Alice in Wonderland after she fell down the rabbit hole. She laughs as her guide speaks to her, reminding her that she enjoys working with metaphor and symbols in the dreamwork she does with her counseling clients. Donald Duck appears next and she chuckles as he teases with her to get her to lighten up: "If it looks like a duck and sounds like a duck, it is a duck."

Faith's guide appears to her as her Divine Child with long curly hair to her waist. She is dressed like an angel and carrying a wand. She taps Faith on the head with her magic wand and says, "You overthink everything!" as she reminds Faith that making decisions has always been difficult for her.

Her Divine Child, an archetype symbolizing innocence and playfulness, goes on to tell her that she's not going to tell Faith what decision to make. She tells her that she can make it or not make it. The things she's trying to do are fine. One is not better than another. She can do all three projects if she sticks around on this planet long enough. And even if she makes a mistake, she's old enough to make a mistake, and it won't matter in the long run whether she gets the story down in a book, builds, or remodels. The indecision is what's causing the issue now as it had in her past incarnations.

In the scene as the witch, even killing the peasant or not wasn't the big issue in the end. Either action brought about someone's death. She wasn't an evil witch; she did a lot of good for the people in the community.

Faith's guide tells her that she worries about money too much and that she should spend time writing her book instead of worrying over what to do. She has the money to spend if she chooses to. Faith admits she has always been overly worried about spending.

Her guide shows her a comparison to the small business owner, who often traveled to Europe for his business. He hadn't been afraid to spend money on things he enjoyed doing. In fact, he considered it an investment. And he benefited from the experience of having done it.

Faith also recognizes others from that life as people she's known in her current life. The angry father who had killed her in the past life is someone she's known and always had an uneasy feeling about. And the man she had freed is an acquaintance who always seemed like a decent guy.

Her guide explains that the purpose of the past life as the witch had been to find who she really was and to have the courage and confidence to act on it. She is briefly shown other past lives where she tried to help people when others didn't approve of her decisions, yet she found the courage to be who she was.

Even in her current life she confesses that she has not always followed her heart's desire. As a young girl she'd purposely give the wrong answers in class to avoid the stigma attached to being a smart girl. And as an adult she faced her share of obstacles with others who were fearful of therapy. She recognized a pattern of wanting to share her gifts with others but feeling held back in some way.

Faith's guide tells her that she won't make the decision for her, that this is something she'll have to figure out for herself. She is there to give guidance but ultimately it is up to Faith to decide what she wants to do.

Faith speaks up with confidence as she says it is time for her to write those stories down and turn them into a book for her children and grandchildren. She already knows how she plans to approach it and arrange them. Next, she decides that although she is passionate about building, it has its drawbacks and that purchasing a smaller house to remodel is the answer. She recognizes that to build or not to build wasn't the issue at hand, that these options were presenting themselves to her to help her resolve her longstanding issue with indecision.

Her guide smiles, cautioning Faith "not to be such a scaredy-cat. No matter what you do, no one's going to take an axe to your throat." Faith chuckles again, seeming lighter, as she repeats this to me. The guide advises Faith it is time to release reluctance and fear of risk in making big decisions. The fear of making the wrong decision holds her back from making *any* decision most of the time.

Upon reflection, Faith recognizes how trying not to act by doing nothing has closed doors for her in her current life. She once believed the Universe had made the path and she was to just follow it as best as she could by not making decisions. Now it is time to change that.

A significant past life for Faith was one as a leader with intelligence and the gift of vision. A respected shaman in a Native American tribe, he trusted and followed his visions to lead his people out west, away from the white man during a pivotal time in Native American history. The tribe blamed him for the loss of their land, but it ultimately saved their lives and allowed them to live on. For the rest of that life, the shaman questioned whether he had made the right decision, and he died feeling as if he had made a mistake. Faith carried this over into her current life, questioning herself constantly whenever faced with a choice.

Her guide assures her she has not made a mistake. There is a bigger plan in place. She is advised that although decisions can be difficult, she is to have the courage to trust her intuition and wisdom and move forward with plans she wants to make. In doing so, the Universe will support her.

Faith's guide, still appearing as her Divine Child, takes her wand with the star on the end of it and touches Faith's forehead with a tap similar to Glinda the Good Witch in *The Wizard of Oz*. And the session ends just like that.

Faith feels as if the longstanding burden she carried has been lifted. She recognizes that whenever it came to decision-making, she worried over which choice to make. In the past she felt as if her choices would affect the tribe in a detrimental way, not considering that they may affect the tribe in a positive way. Her worrying overshadowed her intuition and ability to choose clearly so sometimes choices ended being made for her. When she wasn't focused on worry, she naturally knew what to do. And other times when she didn't act on her intuition, she found out she would have been right, had she followed through.

Just after the session, Faith contacts me to share that this new understanding has shifted her perspective. She's relieved to be working on these projects, knowing that the many decisions that will be involved will be easier without the weight of the worry over decision-making. These projects are a chance to put it to the test.

—— *Soul-Minded Journaling* ——
What Holds You Back from Trusting Yourself?

Many habits are rooted in the emotions. It starts with a reaction that becomes a habitual response, such as not trusting yourself or not taking chances. It can also manifest as falling into the defensive habit of reacting off of others, rather than responding from your core self.

What are some habits you would like to change? Are decisions difficult for you to make? Do you allow others to make decisions for you? Do you hold back when you know what you'd like to do? Dig deep and find the courage to speak up. Start by observing yourself in situations with others. Do you join in? Why not?

Start joining in to conversations with others, instead of being a bystander. Add your thoughts to the conversation, recognizing that your opinions have value too. Notice how others respond. Listen to yourself and to them. Listen to your intuition and the guidance that you're being given. Learn to trust it and to follow it to the amazing places you'll lead.

chapter 9

Letting Go of What Is
No Longer Yours

Sandy shows up a few minutes late for her session. Rushing into the office, she explains, apologetically, she has just gotten out of the shower, thrown on a beach dress, and rushed over to the office with no time left to do her hair and makeup. I tell her not to worry, that no one would see her but me, and after we talk briefly I will dim the lights during the actual hypnosis portion of the session. We laugh, and she seems to relax a bit while we talk about other things. Later, as the session unfolds, it becomes apparent that the woman standing before me is the opposite in nature to the straitlaced character from her own past life that she will explore in today's session.

Sandy wants to explore her past lives because she wants to get clear on some things. She is in a transition period in her life and wants to get clarity. In her meditations when asking for guidance, she gets flashes of past lives. She wants to bring all the pieces together to help her move forward in a spiritually aligned way. She also wants to find out more about a health issue she's been dealing that has started to improve with a new regimen she is under.

We begin the All Lives Session with the usual induction and deepening. Sandy quickly moves through some present life memories as we make our way back through time. She experiences excitement at being born into this life to a loving mother with whom she shares a close relationship early on. Excited to meet her mother and be with her, she enjoys the feeling of her mother's love, knowing that love is reciprocated. To Sandy's great relief, she sees very clearly that her mother is happy as a young wife and mother. She understands that her mother's unhappiness later in life was caused by other factors in the marriage, not Sandy's birth as she had feared. It is a great revelation for her to realize this, and to realize that somehow she has picked up her mother's unhappiness later in life and taken it on as her own.

After crossing through a bright light into an open space at the end of a hallway, Sandy's spirit guide, Nipa, appears to her as an Asian Indian, tall, thin, and graceful, standing in the periphery wearing a sari. She shows Sandy a scene with two children growing to adulthood and then meeting as they became adults. A woman with long brown hair is there in an open field of golden yellow flowers and blue skies standing with her beau. They are both young and their relationship is full of promise, but Sandy feels a rush of great sadness come over her relating to events that are to come.

Fast-forwarding a few years into their marriage, she suddenly feels a pressure on her stomach and a sharp pain as if something is stuck there. It feels as if something is trying to get out, but also something is stuck there too. Nipa shows her the image of a mother and father holding a new baby being christened. It is the young couple from the field. There had actually been two babies, but only one survived. The stillborn child is still inside, stuck there, while its twin has broken free.

The pain is connected to the area just under Sandy's ribs and up to through the lungs and heart. It sits there like a heavy pressure that weighs on her diaphragm and makes it difficult to breathe. Sandy remarks that she experienced a similar pain when she had her first child at about the same age as this woman. Nipa helps her to realize that this was a part of herself that she didn't want to "see," and this memory serves as an entry point to reveal itself to her now that she is ready.

She is shown the point in the past life that is tied to the pain. The pain came about at the birth of her child in her current life, though it was rooted into her past life experiences with loss as a Civil War widow. She and her husband, a Confederate officer in the Civil War, lost their little girl before he went off to war. They each dealt with pain the only way they knew how. Leaving his young wife to grieve the loss of their child alone, he ran away, using the distraction of war to take him away from the constant reminders of his young daughter around their Virginia homeplace. She kept herself occupied and her anger buried deep.

They talked about having other children once the war was over, but they never did. He returned home as a broken man, for which she never forgave him. He later died, which only fueled her bitterness at losing someone else she loved.

The young couple in the field had such a promising future ahead, but all that changed with the death of their child and then the Civil War. It changed her, wore her out from the hardships she and everyone endured. She finally gave up on the idea that life could ever be good again and was bitter and resentful of the injustices life had placed upon her. She lost everyone she loved in that war and now was all alone in the world in a home filled with the belongings of those she has lost. The belongings served as old, painful memories to a life she no longer had—toys, clothing, furniture. She was angry because she considered herself to be a good person and didn't understand why this was happening to her. She didn't deserve this and her life was in ruins.

She would never be happy again, but as a well-to-do proper Southern woman, she held back her words and swallowed her tears instead. She was too proud to reveal her pain, so she kept it stuffed way down inside. The worst of it all was that it was stuffed down so deep that she didn't even know how to let it go if she wanted to. What was the point anyway? After the Civil War ended there was no place to find relief. Everyone was suffering with no way to lift themselves up. Everyone was broken.

Sandy speaks with her past-life counterpart, offering compassion and understanding. The widow's scowled face softens a bit as Sandy starts to make realizations about how this has influenced her current life thinking. Sandy is more of a free spirit than her uptight, straitlaced, past-life counterpart; however, both have experienced suffering nonetheless.

As they talk, the sensation begins to change. At first it is like a clamp, pinching on either side of Sandy's abdomen. In her chest there is a hardness like a lead bullet lodged there in her heart. As the light of awareness begins to reveal what Sandy needs to see, a golden yellow light pours into this space.

The bullet opens like a flower as each of the petal-like layers begins to unfold up to the light. And as they continue to talk, it continues to shift. Layers and layers of pain and associations between current life and past life similarities begin shifting. A few moments later, light sprays out of the top like fireworks, just as tears of relief spring from Sandy's eyes.

She smiles proudly as these new discoveries about herself sink in. Sandy recalls making the decision early on in her current life to not be so disciplined that she is chained into a "straitjacket kind of life." Others have made her out to be wrong for choosing her own path in life. She recognizes that her free-spiritedness isn't a bad thing after all.

As Sandy and the Civil War widow finish talking, the Civil War widow is led into the light to join a group of souls who are there waiting for her. Many of the loved ones she believed to be lost reunite with her to welcome her home.

Sandy's attention is drawn to a Greek-styled building with columns. She follows the pebbled path, lined with roses and flowers, that takes her to the entrance. Her guide, Nipa, steps out of one of the columns to greet her. More is revealed to Sandy about the Civil War life. Nipa reminds her that every life has seeds of pain in it. One must accept that and not run away from it. She tells Sandy to take the lessons in stride and to not hide from them.

Sandy feels herself being lifted up by the love Nipa has for her. Nipa reassures Sandy that she is proud of her. She encourages Sandy to continue opening herself up and to not be so cautious. Nipa projects her golden light, with touches of purple and bronze, onto Sandy, showing her how to open herself up.

Nipa shares with Sandy that she chose to appear as an Indian woman in today's session because Sandy has taken an interest in Hindu and Buddhist mantras lately. It is her way to honor Sandy for opening up to learning.

Another insight comes relating to the pain in the abdomen. Humans are like batteries that plug into each other's energy fields. Be mindful of people who drain us and those who energize us, and in the reverse, whether we're energizing or draining to others. Sandy is told not to take things others say or do so personally. She doesn't have to "carry" everyone's emotional pain in her solar plexus. She recognizes how her gift of being intuitive opens her to feeling others' pain. It also causes her to feel responsible to help them and it is adversely affecting her health.

Nipa reminds Sandy that the pain is not even hers. It is someone else's... family, friends, clients... Sandy is instructed to use her gift of being able to recognize where the issue in them lies, so she can send them to someone who can help them. That itself is helping them.

Nipa explains further that Sandy cannot "fix" the pain for *them* by holding it in *her* abdomen. Sandy holding the pain only causes her pain but doesn't resolve their pain for them. This robs them of their own abilities to "fix" the pain themselves. Sandy shares that as a young girl, she wished that she could take on her mother's pain. Even at a young age, she knew that no matter how much she wished she could heal it, her mother was the only one that could do that. She is not responsible for her mother's happiness.

As the pieces come together for Sandy, she feels ready to take on the next phase of her life. She is reminded that she doesn't have to go it alone; there will be others there to help her along the way. She feels a sense of renewal, relief, and spiritual alignment at being released from the pain of the Civil War widow. She has faith that more will be revealed in time by working more closely with her guide and her spiritual team.

—— *Soul-Minded Exercise* ——
Cutting the Cords Visualization, and Clear Clutter to Ease the Mind

As part of learning to let go of what is not yours, it's important to take a look at the people and things you surround yourself with. There comes a time when it's necessary to let go of certain people or things that are no longer serving you. Clearing distractions and unnecessary drama keep you more connected to your soul's guidance, allowing you to move more smoothly along your path.

Part 1: Cutting the Cords

For this two-part exercise, it's important first to take a look at key relationships in your life. Do you have healthy boundaries with others? Are you carrying their pain as your own? Do you try to "fix" it for them? Take a moment to identify the people in your life whose cord it's time to cut—those people who drain your energy, or you drain theirs. Cutting the cords doesn't have to mean letting them go from your life. It can mean letting go of energy the way it is so that you can create a new approach to the relationship.

Identify the people (living or deceased) you need to cut the cords to. This doesn't have to be face-to-face; this is an energetic clearing exercise that works across time and space. Then close your eyes and imagine the energetic cord that runs from you to them. Notice where that "plugs in to" your body. There may be many cords or one big one. Now imagine a golden pair of scissors cutting through those cords, freeing you both from these emotional entanglements. Surround them with light and thank them for being in your life and for what they've taught you about yourself as you let them go. Let the light move into the spaces in your body and mind, healing the areas where the cords were attached.

If the person is someone you'd like to keep in your life, but have a healthier relationship with, imagine having a conversation with them as if they're sitting across from you. Again, they don't have to be face-to-face. Come from your heart and imagine telling them that you'd like to continue to have them in your life, but in a better way that supports each of you. Let them know you're sorry for any interference you created by trying to "fix" them. You can also let them know that you don't need fixing. You'll figure out your issues too. Notice the subtle changes that take place in the relationship over time.

Part II: Clear the Clutter to Ease the Mind

Next, sort through physical possessions to determine what to keep and what to let go of. It's easy to get caught up in keeping material objects that once held meaning to us, but then over time these items can become painful reminders of the past. Broken things become a reminder of things that need to be repaired every time you look at them, and if they start to pile up, it can feel overwhelming and trap your energy, creating stagnation. Storing unneeded items or old, worn-out clothing takes up space and costs money to clean and maintain.

Are you grieving the loss of someone, or a relationship that's over, and holding on to the pain of this loss by holding on to material things that remind you of them? Do the things around you empower you when you see them, or do they cause more pain? Do they leave you feeling uplifted or downtrodden? Do you even like them or feel like you "should" keep them because you loved the person they used to belong to?

Go through your home and remove the things that you no longer need or use, or that you are holding on to out of guilt or some other disempowering emotion.

Make a pile for items to be repaired, replaced, sold, donated, or discarded. If the items that you'd like to get rid of have family connections, pass them on to others in the family, but you don't have to give them space in your own home if they're not meaningful or useful to you. Sort through clothing you don't or can't wear any longer. Find someone who will enjoy these items!

Notice how freeing it feels to clear the clutter from your space and your mind. This freedom allows room for the new people and things that will be coming into your life!

chapter 10
Spiritual Rehabilitation
for Injured Souls

Juniper wants to find answers to questions she has regarding a sense of not belonging. She is a free spirit. Others in her life who are very traditional in their thinking are often judgmental and critical of her beliefs, which causes her to feel discouraged for not fitting in.

She has not come for a session to question the afterlife or whether there even is an afterlife. She wants to find out more about her purpose in life and why she came to Earth to begin with. She feels there is something else she is to do beyond raising her children, which she enjoys very much. Something is calling her, and she wants to understand more about what it is. She hopes that today's SESR session will provide more insight into the answers she seeks.

Moving through her soul's history, she makes a few stops in her current life that are needed to clear issues surrounding grief. These are significant because losing several close friends at a young age has left her feeling disconnected from those around her, and contributes to her sense of not belonging. Part of the reason for this is, of course, missing her friends who have passed, and the other reason is the way that those around her have chosen to deal with death. Sometimes they don't know what to say, or are insensitive in the way they approached her about the loss.

Juniper stops over in the womb, where she feels very connected to her life. She feels a sense of innocence in a strong, capable body. She notices that her mind is open, yet somewhat fanciful. She comments that as a young girl, mystical things always made more sense to her than people and relationships; she was confused about why people acted the way they did.

Being a mother herself, it is wonderful for Juniper to re-experience the warmth of her mother's love and her joy at being pregnant. Juniper's father is happy about the pregnancy too. He is also surprised that Juniper is coming so quickly after her brother; he had hoped they'd have a little longer to prepare before having another child.

In the womb, Juniper feels strong and capable, knowing she is coming to help people remember. Her purpose is to serve as a touchstone to the "other side" to help them remember, in order to bring healing through these memories. Her guide explains that people will naturally be drawn to her because they can sense this about her.

Additionally, she understands that part of the dynamic she has chosen for herself this time around is to go it alone to learn how to maneuver the twists and turns of life. At a certain level, souls have and need less guidance, so this is a natural part of her soul's evolution. Of course, help is available, but at times she feels lost, seemingly without a teacher to guide her and she will have to figure it out herself.

She has chosen a family who will love her, but not always understand her. She knows she won't have that kind of emotional support from them. She hopes that she can help them to gain a broader vision, and that maybe they will come to understand her better because of it.

While in the womb her soul is able to come and go right up until the birth. She describes it as a sense of freedom where she can fly fast in the expansiveness of the clouds and communicate fully with her spiritual team in the cosmic realm. It is a last chance to be free and unencumbered before she squeezes herself into a tiny package for the final joining, like a lightning bolt fusing the soul and body together just before the birth process will begin.

She comments that like all the lives she has lived on Earth, she doesn't like the denseness there. She starts out as a brilliant light but feels whittled away. This mind and body are a good fit with her soul's consciousness, but the emotional system requires rebalancing when she has to interact with the people. It is frustrating being in this human form, trying to work with the people. Sometimes Juniper gets caught up in a wave of emotion because this brain is programmed in an overly fanciful way to keep her from "forgetting" completely about life on the other side. This makes it more difficult to relate to others or fall into place with them, while not wanting to get caught up in games people play.

The brain is an important part of the balancing process; however, when these systems get overloaded, it's more difficult for it to return to balance. Juniper needs to take time to disconnect from those around her to restore the much-needed balance to herself. Although she is afraid she is being frivolous, she is reassured it's a vital component to her emotional and overall state of well-being. Balance is important for keeping everything running smoothly.

The journey along Juniper's soul's history leads her to a past life in the late 1800s as a seven-year-old boy named Jushen who lived in a village in the mountains of Asia. It was daytime as he found himself standing in front of a temple that was surrounded by prayer flags. He was wrapped in a deep, red-colored outfit, and stood with other dark-eyed boys dressed the same way. Their brown skin had a ruddy complexion to it from the dry, cold climate of the mountains.

Jushen and the other boys were in training to become Tanjian monks. The young monks were chosen by the older monks at a very young age and brought to the temple. Jushen described this with mixed feelings. "It was sad to leave my parents," he said, "but it's an honor to be chosen." The sacrifice was worth it for the greater good of others.

Once inside the prayer temple, the energy and warmth filled the space, in contrast to the cold stoniness of the floor. Woven mats were placed on the stone floor for each child with a big prayer wheel on either side with space between them. "We're taken care of. There is love and compassion here," the young monk commented. "This is where I spend my days."

As he became a teenager, Jushen's job was to work with the earth. Not much grew in the rocky garden soil just outside the temple. He often went outside to gaze over the mountaintop, curious about the rest of the world beyond his view. It's about perspective, Jushen said. "I'm far up on this hill with all this sight, but I'm not really a part of what I'm able to see. My teachers who are kind and patient have lived their whole life here. I'm happy here but it's a different kind of happy. For me it's more like a sense of duty and satisfaction. It's a feeling of fullness from committing to that. It's a life of introspection within myself. It's a chance to pull worlds together in my mind like a bridge."

The monks lived high atop the mountain, which was a difficult place for people to travel. Occasionally people brought supplies to the temple, and there were a few families scattered on the outskirts that the monks helped when someone died or was sick; this kept the monks from feeling permanently and purposely cut off from everyone. There was great respect here. People who came there did so without disrupting the balance because they respected it.

As Jushen grew older, many of his teachers were older or had died. He and several other monks took on the role of teaching the children. It was the way of keeping the old traditions alive, the same as he had been brought up.

At the end of that life, Jushen died on the mountaintop as an old man in his early seventies, the same as his teachers had before him. He was surrounded by the children he had helped, who were now adults guiding the next generation of young monks along the path to monkhood. He was proud of them and the work they were doing. He died feeling content having lived a simple life that had been about the work, the sacrifice, and the discipline.

Crossing into the spirit world, Jushen sheds the body of the disciplined monk and feels the freedom of his spirit expand beyond the boundaries of his earthly body. His spirit is greeted by his guide who embraces him and says, "Good to see you...." They have known one another forever and are on an equal level with one another. Getting down to business right away, his guide says, "Glad you're back; there's a lot of work to do with displaced souls."

Right away Juniper is shown an image of someone in a healing box among chambers of healing boxes where the displaced souls are put to be healed and renewed. She informs me that she works here. These souls remain here a few hundred years (in Earth time), or sometimes forever, to be looked after like a kind of spiritual rehabilitation center. Juniper is like a "soul doctor" for extreme souls. She oversees the rehabilitation process of the injured souls to make sure that they are healing properly.

With no time to waste, she goes directly to her "office," which is equipped with a shower where she quickly showers off the "stuff" from her earthly life. She puts on her white lab coat and picks up her clipboard while those she left in charge bring her up to date on the state of things while she was away.

It's fascinating to hear her talk about how she's worked with the injured souls for millennia. She discusses it quite matter-of-factly as if it were just another day at the office. She describes how she uses these "trips" to Earth as a way to stay checked in to the human condition and for learning to work with the dense energies on Earth. Upon returning to the rehabilitation center following these trips, she takes a quick light shower in her own quarters to be refreshed. She goes on to describe these showers as being like warm, non-sticky honey that runs down her soul body to release the dense energies. She says that "sometimes it can get confusing when I incarnate because of the dark energies of Earth. It's like taking their 'stuff' home from the office with me."

There's an intensity to the work Juniper does in the spirit world. "It still has a quality of pain to it," she says, "a correlation of having done the work here. I can feel the pain there. I have to hold on to threads of it when working with extreme souls, so I can keep a handle on what I'm doing and what they're doing." She explains that "the souls in the boxes are mostly male, masculine incarnated souls. They are the serial killers, mass murderers, and those who have lost their connection." Juniper's soul works with them, doing a kind of energetic therapy. Part of that therapy involves her just being with them. She makes contact with these souls to help them to re-establish their soul connection.

Each ward of the rehab center is laid out differently, and there are different jobs for different wards. Not everyone is allowed contact with these souls, nor are these souls allowed contact with one another. Juniper goes into their space to explore and study them. "I choose to view them as my children," she explains. "The close contact I provide them helps directly with the reconnection."

Juniper's soul works closely with her guide. While she's on Earth, her guide is a point of connection to her work at the rehab center in the spirit world. She recognizes other spirits who pass through this hospital-like place. They float by, saying "welcome back" as they return to their wing of the center to do their own work.

After "work," Juniper goes to her own cottage within a small community to rest and renew her energy. Upon deciding to go there, she is immediately transported there. It's a beautiful stone cottage with a permeating sense of peace. She goes there alone, while those who she's closest to reside nearby like neighbors in the woods. "Although it feels like we're all a group, each of us is an individual. Although we all want to be around one another, we don't reside in the same place," she explains. "We all 'will' our own place of peace. We've constructed these sanctuaries because of the work that we do."

Juniper uses the energy from the cottage to keep her own soul's energy balanced. The special stones that make the structure offer a different form of healing vibration for restorative balance. This place contains the things she needs that she creates and places around her, such as the woods and ocean. Finding those same things on Earth is beneficial. It's not a luxury, it's necessary for her; she also needs to let go and enjoy life more. She is reminded of this again, as she was in the womb segment of our session, because it's important that she find time for this on Earth.

This is more of an individual track for a soul, rather than being a part of or doing the same things as most souls in this world. It's not easy to do. She knows that this is where much of her sense of not belonging comes from in her incarnations.

Momentarily reflecting on the life as the monk, Juniper recognizes that some of her current life feelings of separation stem from that life, but knows it was important to bring the remembrance of Jushen's life in with her to assist with her current life mission. It makes sense to her now that what is lacking in her current life is the respect for one another that had been so abundant in the life on top of the mountain.

Her guide reminds her that she doesn't have to isolate herself from others during her incarnations, but this specialty work is difficult to drop suddenly when she incarnates on Earth. "It's like I'm bringing 'baggage' with me when I incarnate, rather than the other way around," she says. "People are drawn to me and then put off by my non-traditional beliefs. This is a direct correlation to the work in the spirit world with my job being rehabilitation of damage. I'm going to attract things that need repair. But when it's attracted on this realm, people are afraid, though being drawn toward it … there's a lack of understanding and acceptance."

Next, beings lead Juniper to an area in the spirit world that goes from lightness to darkness to show how darkness is really pain. They reveal this as a denser side of injury. "Denser, lower, and mysterious, but still it's pain," they advise her. "People [in human form] want relief. They want to be heard. They are drawn to the other side out of their desire for light." Juniper's soul in its various incarnations helps to bring light into their world.

She informs me that she has a different understanding of darkness now. "Dark intentions or any sort of work done with the perception that it's being done out of malice can be considered darkness … it can also be a feeling of being off track or misguided." This is different than someone like a soldier who is required to kill in order to keep others safe. Her work with extreme souls is with those souls who cross the line. "It's an expression of the soul to decide to go to a place that is labeled as dark, but it's exploration. It's just another facet of our individual journey and exploration into what's possible."

When I ask if serial killers incarnate with this intent, she tells me that serial killers do not incarnate with the intent to be that. They get off track with their soul's mission upon incarnating. Something changes in their soul's personality within their human mind that makes them more susceptible to this behavior. It's as if a spark is ignited at some point, like a fire that these souls decide not to put out. What feels like massive, uncontrolled injury and pain to them is a form of a lost connection.

Juniper and others work to restore the connection by starting from the beginning. It's a process of reparenting the soul and taking it back to its origins. She explains that she's not afraid and she doesn't love them any less. She works with them on an energetic level to nurture them and hold them to get them back to a stable place. There's no rush. It takes a great deal of time to achieve this. It also takes a great deal of energy from Juniper, such that coming to Earth sometimes feels like a break from this intense work.

After spending much of the session learning about her role in the spirit world, it is time to visit with the Elders. She remarks that the Elders consist of an eclectic mix from different places. One leads the meeting and reminds Juniper to "go slow, don't be so concerned with the need to progress in a certain way on Earth or to meet certain expectations." She is to remember what she has come here to do and to facilitate it. It's important for her to be part of a community where she'll find the support she needs. It's not all about the work, it's also about enjoying life more, and the work will still get done. There's a tendency to want to go in and do the work so the work can all be over, but that's not how it works. It's important to have a life and maintain that deep connection.

Juniper comments how she's surrounded by people who are stuck, and seeing them that way is stressful to her. It's difficult to see them living in such a small way, but she's reminded that they all have their lessons to learn, and hurting is a part of that. She is told she can help them better from a distance by not being so involved. The Elders reassure her that she is doing fine; she should not be afraid to be more a part of things. It's part of the human experience to be vulnerable. In fact, it's okay.

Juniper is given a glimpse of her future where she sees herself feeling more solid in being herself. She releases things she no longer needs and along with that will come a sense of liberation. She is shown her husband supporting these changes as they downsize their lives. They will travel and explore exciting places. She sees her children are happy with fewer things and enjoying the company of friends. In doing this, her children will get the lesson that what's simple is what's most important.

As a gift, the Elders show Juniper that the world is in the palm of her hand. They tell her that she has all that she needs on Earth as they hand her a crystal ball that fits perfectly into the palm of her hand to use for clarity and for vision. She sees herself opening up more and letting in more information and light. They tell her that opening to the small things taking place around her will bring in the light. She is shown other beings around her "minding their own business." Using her gift of perception, she will tune in to the subtleties more clearly now as a constant reminder of the magic that is taking place on all levels and remember that we are not the only thing happening right now.

The Elders advise Juniper that what she had thought is a fanciful way of looking at things is more accurate than she realizes. She doesn't need to change who she is just because others around her can't see what she does. She can use this energy to help them expand.

Juniper's soul group's first incarnation was not on Earth, which leads me to ask further about the workings of other levels with one another, specifically if there are ETs in the spirit world. One of the Elders, who is an ET, comes forward and responds, "It isn't that we're separate, it's just that we're individual and different. We all have a planet of origin that resonates with our vibration and we just take on that role and that costume while we reside there … extraterrestrials were created with different gifts, different ways of relating, and different things to offer."

He informs Juniper (and me) that they're wired differently, with a different vibration, and their costume is easily accessible and easy to differentiate. "It's like how you can tell it's them, just like a doctor dresses like a doctor or a monk wears his robe," she says. "We are 'them' when we are home. Our planet of origin or where we spend most of our time feels more comforting and is an easier place to be."

Before wrapping up, Juniper is reassured that she is capable. Working in the ward with the damaged souls is like an "internship" before she progresses to the next level. In doing this work on the ground level there is faster healing for all. Her spiritual team reassures her that they know this work is not easy and she doesn't have to go it alone. The crystal ball will help her to stay connected with them, and whenever she feels alone, it will serve as a reminder that she is not. In other lifetimes she didn't need this connection, but times have changed.

Lastly, she's reminded that just as it's important to connect with others, it's important for her to nurture the compassion, to experience and to allow her energy to flow. "Don't stifle it," they tell her; it's vital to her current life's mission as a touchstone to help people remember.

With that, this long session ends. Juniper is tired and excited all at the same time. She needs time to let this settle, but she feels good about the valuable insights and answers she has received. A little over a year after her session, she contacts me to let me know that her husband had been offered a wonderful job opportunity in a foreign country. They sold their belongings, packed up the kids, and decided to see the world from the perspective of a different country and culture.

Many of the worries she once had about how to fulfill her life's mission are gone. She has taken training on a new career path and made a plan for herself that will allow her to set her own hours around her family's schedule and their needs, to do the work she so desperately feels called to do. She can do all of this while enjoying a life in a beautiful country where the pace is slower and new adventures lie ahead. The crystal ball in the palm of her hand remains a reminder to her of how work doesn't have to feel like work; it can be fun too!

—— *Soul-Minded Exercise* ——
Create Your Peaceful Place

Everyone needs a place to unwind when they get home at the end of the day. Creating a calming atmosphere around you can transport you from the stresses of daily life and help you to relax, when it's done with awareness. If others live with you, then choose an area you can work with. It doesn't have to be the entire house; it could be that you redo a bathroom to enjoy relaxing in the tub, or bring a chair into the bedroom for a quiet spot to read or listen to music. For others, the den is their sanctuary, so make it relaxing for you and your family. For some, their special place may be the back porch.

Journal for a moment the things you like, such as colors you find pleasant and relaxing. Look around your home to the things that surround you. Do you see things you like around you? If yes, what are they? If no, why not? What vibe does your home give off? Peaceful or chaotic?

Create a special space in your home to unwind by bringing together your favorite things from nature—like gemstones, essential oils, plants, salt lamps, music, etc. Bring in elements of earth, wind, water, and fire. Choose décor with your favorite colors, or from your favorite artist or photographer. The color you choose is important. It can feel calming or keep you keyed up depending on the color you choose. Create or find an outdoor space too.

Now sit in your relaxing space and take a look at yourself: where are your dark areas, injuries? What are you afraid of uncovering?

Take a look at the people in your life with a new perspective. Are you surrounded by people but not being authentic to yourself? Are you too isolated? Do you need to be a part of a community?

Are you having fun in your life? What could you do to bring more fun into your life?

Journal your findings and learn to heal these with light, fun, and joy.

chapter 11
Patience, Trust, and Spirituality

Mira has a great life. She is happily married, and things are going well for her family. Both she and her husband are successful in their chosen professions. She enjoys her job as a consultant and takes great pride in her work.

She is having a difficult time, though, because her insecurities are getting the best of her. Rather than enjoying her hard-earned success, she has a fear of it, and a fear of standing out from the crowd; however, both her career and her husband's cause her to draw attention to herself. She also admits to having an irrational fear of betrayal by her mate although she has no evidence to this effect. She wants to explore the root of this further, so she can feel more secure and put it to rest.

She also wants to understand why she tries to rush through her "lessons" in her current life so she could hurry up and "go home." Meditation is a way of life in her culture, but sometimes her spiritual beliefs take her out of the moment and into her head, causing her to overthink things. Her multifaceted upbringing had given her strong connections to spiritual teachers such as Babaji, Ganesh, Shiva, Durga, and Jesus.

Mira goes under very easily as the All Lives Regression begins. Just after the induction process, she notices a thick, carved wooden door with Asian designs on it. The door opened, and she feels a pair of big, glowing hands holding hers.

A scene quickly emerged of Mira in India as a dark-skinned male with a thick mustache, wearing a gold crown on his head. It was around the year 500. He was sitting on a white horse with a beautiful golden saddle across it and beautiful glowing gold all around him. He asked to be addressed as "Raja" which is Sanskrit for king.

Raja was holding a flag across his chest, while leading a procession past a temple and down a street paved in gold. The street was lined with crowds of people who had come to see him. Although it was his birthright to be king, Raja didn't like the attention being put upon him.

Raja's kingdom was doing very well under his administration. He was well liked, had a good sense of humor, and his people were happy. His wealth afforded him a beautiful palace for him, his wives, and twelve children—eight boys and four girls. He was pleased with his queen, who was mother to three of his children.

We moved through the life rather quickly, seemingly rushing to get to the end, stopping at a significant point where Raja sat on his throne with his trusted advisors beside him. Soul Recognition revealed Mira's present-day spouse as one of the trusted advisors. Someone from neighboring lands was upset over a land dispute. Raja listened intently, hoping to mitigate the situation without the need to go to war. Unfortunately, war was imminent.

The warring nations fought one another, and many people died. In the end, Raja's kingdom won the war. Raja survived but was hurt and limping, and one of his eyes had been burned permanently shut. Over time, surrounded by good physicians, his legs began to improve, but this experience changed Raja.

Not long after this, Raja was finished with administration. He retired and gave up his kingdom to his nephew, in whom he had a lot of confidence. In hindsight, he wished he had spent more time with his sons, teaching them to run a kingdom so he could have turned it over to one of them. His kingdom continued to prosper.

Raja was an old man now. Without the responsibilities of a kingdom to run, he spent most of his time meditating in the forest. He had a little hut built in a clearing where he enjoyed sitting in solitude for most of the day. After the war, he felt he just had to get away from it all. He enjoyed the simplicity of this place.

This is where he died. His last thoughts were of what a good life that had been. He liked being in charge of things. As Raja's spirit leaves his body and crosses over into the spirit world, Mira describes it as looking like aurora borealis but with a lot of gold!

She is greeted by her spiritual teacher, Babaji, who has been with her throughout many of her incarnations, and who helps her with her spiritual side. She smiles when she sees him. Several other spiritual teachers appear, too, sending her supportive energy and reminding her there is only love. As they do this, Babaji shifts into Shiva, whom she recognizes by his eyes.

She explains that she shares guides with others and that guides can look after several people at once. At a certain level of a soul's evolution, there are fewer guides to tap into. Universal guidance is available to be accessed by all, it's not "claimed" by any one person. It's not really accurate to say "my guides," but we do.

As souls reach higher levels of experience, guides don't have to be named like they are at the lower levels. A more experienced soul works with the spiritual guide they're meant to work with by tuning into their energy and vibration, and in return the spirit guide connects with them. Guides distribute a portion of their energy, which is given a name that is vibrational to what one needs, so they can relate to it and to the guidance given. It's part of soul energy distribution. Names equate to a guide's energy and to one's soul understanding of the situation.

As an aside, this helped to explain those times in session when I ask a client their guide's name, and they either don't get a name or a guide laughs and says, "Just call me 'Bob.'" Guides' names reflect what the client needs at that time, such as a specific quality or a reminder of a significant past life.

There are many spiritual teachers here. Some work more closely with Mira than others. They communicate directly with her, transmitting knowledge to her through images with embedded meaning. There are different guides for different needs.

Her spiritual teachers are helping her to advance by bringing her energy up to the next level. They show her an image of a hiker climbing through different atmospheres on the way to the top of a mountain. She explains that shifting energy to the next level is like going through the atmosphere, through waves of colors to get to the top. Each wave is a different color and the colors keep changing. Each wave moves through her like an energy that activates knowledge at the cellular level.

She sees a male figure helping souls along to the next level and reaching up to a brilliant light that he guides them toward. Mira feels him sending energy that opens her heart. She says she had closed it and protects it too much but needs to open it now. The lyrics of a song come into her mind and tears of joy stream down her face as she reaches the peak of the mountain.

Her spiritual teachers explain to her that it's not time for her to go back "home" yet; she has lessons to learn here on Earth. She discovers that patience is one of the current life lessons she's currently working on. Her spouse is helping her with this. Mira is instructed to connect with the mountain whenever she needs to strengthen her spiritual connection while she learns patience.

Babaji showers Mira with a peace-filled light. After a long pause, she advises me that Babaji is a guide in the middle level between the ones with no names and the ones with names. Next, he shows her an animated image of feathered skeletons with hearts. She laughs as she realizes that it's a metaphor for how souls are like birds that can soar high.

Next, Mira is guided to the Soul Reflection area to take a look at the lessons from the life as Raja. She reveals that Raja had a skill for showing others in his kingdom ways to improve their lives for the better. He had a knack for knowing the right thing to do for people to help them. During most of that life he focused on his kingdom and less on his family. Babaji praises Raja for walking away from ruling the kingdom. He achieved the goals that were set for that life, but he could have spent more time with his children and taught them, so they could have been better rulers like his nephew. He could have kept the balance of a spiritual life and still had fun.

The fear Mira has of standing out in a crowd stems from this lifetime as Raja. Her spiritual team instructs her not to fear success, but to keep the balance. Raja disliked the fame. They advise her that fame is coming into her life again with the success of a family member. It's another chance for a lesson she's to learn. It's important she find the balance by keeping her heart open to avoid going into ego. Staying in a place of love, not fear, will allow this to happen.

More spiritual teachers appear. First Lakshmi, the goddess of wealth, who assures that she will prosper. Parvati, the goddess of love, and Saraswati, goddess of wisdom and learning, join her. They spread love in front of Mira, telling her to be open to them and they'll help her with the earthly world.

As we finish up the All Lives Regression in prep for her SESR the next day, the birds with the hearts are a reminder that a bird can go low and can go high, showing Mira the heights she can reach if she continues to connect with them. She leaves contemplating the guidance her spiritual teachers have shared with her.

The next morning Mira arrives excited about what lies ahead. We talk for a few minutes and begin the session right away. She goes under easily and moves to a time in the womb when she has the fluidity to come and go prior to being born. Her spirit leaves the developing body, going directly to be with the Sages to get knowledge about the impending life. She passes through a dark sky with tiny dots like stars scattered about. The Sages, appearing as stars, begin writing an animated message for her to see. The message is "patience" with an arrow pointing up like a line. It is glowing as it hits the atmosphere and looks like a rocket in the sky. The tail of the arrow has a cord that runs to a past life where her concerns with betrayal are rooted.

A deeper meaning emerges about her quest to evolve in the spirit realms. "I have to be of this Earth to go higher there," she shared. They advise her that her impatience comes from wanting to get through this life so fast to go "home." She's told to embrace this world if she wants to evolve. No more rushing through life to get through it. She needs to be grounded to reach for the stars. They show her an image of an electric eel touching Earth, lighting it up like fireworks when she follows their advice. She can be charged up with the excitement of reaching the stars, like the eel is charged up with electricity, if she remembers to stay grounded in her daily life.

The purpose of her current incarnation is to touch people and foster their growth. She does this by being herself. Interacting with others, whether in her business or personal life, helps Mira's clients and it helps her. She tends to incarnate as male because of the strong physical bodies and the camaraderie they share. This time she chose to be female to embrace feminine qualities such as sensuality and love, to discover she can be strong and still be loving.

There's the power of sensuality in a relationship. She is to learn to be secure as her female self. People are naturally drawn to her energy. It's revealed that the brain in this female body is designed for an easy connection to the spiritual realms for meditation, which allows her to easily withdraw to the spiritual realms to recharge when needed.

From here, a current gently guides Mira through a spirit door that takes her to another metaphorical scene in ancient times, with small waves rolling up on a beach. Her spirit inhabits a translucent, lion-like creature with a mane, hairy legs, and claws, but which lacks the gracefulness of a lion. He slinks along the sand with one leg in the water and one on the sand where the water hits. He is the leader of the pack. They are hungry and searching for food. As they come upon a translucent hedgehog, they spread out to surprise their prey. After eating, they play together and have fun without the worries of what will come next. His gracefulness returns once he plays.

A guide shows up; all she can see are his eyes. He doesn't have a name, only a message for her. He explains that the lion is symbolic of the wisdom she is hunting. The wisdom is there, but she is next to it. All she must do is jump in to get it. Just swim in it for it to be hers. Sitting in the waters of spirituality she is to not be afraid or impatient, she's to be connected and not worry so much about things. Overthinking spiritual matters has caused a bit of a conundrum, rather than flowing with the natural order of things.

As she embraces this message, light begins streaming in and she finds herself coming upon the spirit cities formed around a mountaintop like clouds. Mira is taken to the valley below where she is greeted by a man, like a priest but dressed in a wizard's hat and robes of bear and alpaca. She intuitively knows that the bear's strong energy represents the wisdom and strength in enjoying the sweetness of life, and alpaca is symbolic of not rushing into things.

Several others are gathered and Mira recognizes them as people she has been in her other incarnations. She admits that some of those times she didn't use her religious powers well. Although she reached a lot of people, she misused her power. The priest advises her that in time she will know more and reassures her that she's learned the lesson and will not do that again. This was the cause for her spiritual performance anxiety, dipping her toe in the water but not completely jumping in.

Next, Babaji guides her from the valley up to the peak of the mountain, where she can see the other peaks from this vantage point. Ten Sages join them there. They are her Soul Advisory Council who appear as Sages. The same Sages stay with her throughout most of her lifetimes. The Sages show her a glowing ball and tell her they are proud of her and all she's accomplished.

They discuss her concerns regarding betrayal. The trigger for betrayal is rooted in a past life. They show her an image of "crying eyes": her own and of someone she has hurt. The fear of betrayal is actually a fear of abandonment from a lifetime in which she rejected her husband and pushed him away. Its purpose has been in opening doors to her heart, allowing her to be more understanding of other people's mistakes and shortcomings. They remind her that she's done it to others and they've done it to her in the past, but now she's broken the pattern. It's bad karma and she's not taking that on this time around.

She explains further that in that past life she and her husband lived in a tiny hut with a thatched roof. He was mostly a good husband but was weighed down by the responsibility of taking care of her and their two boys. Strife between them caused him to become frustrated and caused his drinking to increase. Before it escalated, she was critical of him and rejected him. In frustration, he finally left and found comfort with other women before settling down with one. She was left to go it alone with all the responsibility on her shoulders, scrounging up food for the boys. They both died unhappy at the end of that life.

Sometimes you learn by losing what you have. In hindsight she could see that she didn't accept his love. Her rejection, along with his own issues, ultimately pushed him to leave when he didn't want to go, and she didn't want him to. When she was in that life, she couldn't see it clearly and neither could he. The lesson for her was that her strength was in her love. She didn't help matters by being critical rather than using her positive feminine side. He has his own lessons to work through having been rejected by the woman he loved.

The Sages tell her to relax and enjoy all of life, its ups and its downs. She's not to get drawn into karma or create more for herself. She's been feeling responsible and it's time to let go. They have both learned their lessons from that past life. She's to trust who she is and to not react so much to what others around her do. She can be strong by being loving. The message they have for her is not to give her power over to worries of betrayal or let her ego get in the way. They add, "It could be, and it couldn't be; but you can only change yourself."

This time around, she can take the lessons of love from both the past life of rejection and betrayal, and from Raja, the king, to enjoy life and be present in her life in a loving way without fear of the unknown. By doing so, she'll avoid many of the things she's feared. That's the spiritual way here on Earth. She's learning to accept love as well as give it. She replies, "If I take love in, it expands my chest and I'm able to give more love. Learning to take is part of learning to give. You can't do one without the other."

The Sages are like the mountains in our prior session: she can connect with them anytime she needs to strengthen her spiritual connection. They light up a message in the sky for her that says, "Be you!" It's time for her to relax and enjoy life without the self-scrutiny she had in the past. Being spiritual is being present and in the moment with what is.

As the session closes, she sees eyes again. "They've got their 'eye' on me," she says, amused by this. "I'm watching you. Remember you are loved!" They show her the spirit city on the mountain and tell her to let go of feeling like she needs to go home to be with them. There is time enough for that later; for now, she's to be here, on Earth.

Before ending the session, the Sages do one more thing: they pluck the cord from the arrow that was connected to the past life of rejection and betrayal in the hut. This releases the worry from Mira and the fear of the "unknown." She feels vibrations moving through her as this occurs.

After the session, Mira feels lighter and better. She has a lot to take in and a greater awareness of her soulful qualities that are guiding her in daily life. She recognizes that worry is the opposite of trusting in spirit. Being secure in herself will help her live her purpose. She can recognize her gifts and be more present, by relaxing and enjoying the moment more.

Not long afterward, Mira contacts me, saying that it is all slowly seeping in. She realized afterward how "ungrounded" worrying had caused her to be. She is inhabiting her body more fully, which makes her feel more trusting and connected to her spiritual self. That is the true nature of spirituality. The conscious switch to tea in the evenings is a nice change and a reminder of her connection to the Sages.

—— *Soul-Minded Exercise* ——
Candle Meditation with Gemstones
for Connection and Guidance

Show me the way forward … we all have our moment of doubt or uncertainty. It often comes just before new opportunities are launched. When you find yourself uncertain of what to do next, rest your weary spirit, and connect with your soul directly or through your spiritual team to ask for help finding balance to be spirituality-aligned and more present in your life.

An easy method for learning to tune in to your inner awareness and soul's guidance is through the Candle Meditation.

Set your intention for the meditation. Whether it's to relax or ask a question, get clear before you begin.

Light a candle and relax as you gaze into its flame. Put your focus onto the beautiful colors of the flame dancing, letting distracting thoughts drift away. (Instead of a candle, you can use an object, like a salt, selenite, or pink quartz lamp, or a spot on the wall to focus on.) Soften your focus as you continue to look at the flame (or light from the lamp).

Let your breathing take you to a place of calmness with each exhale. Relax. Allow yourself to just be in this inwardly focused space for a while.

As you bring your awareness inward, connect with your soul or spiritual team by inviting them to come forward. Continue to breathe and notice what you feel. Ask "What would you have me do next?"

Be patient. Notice what feelings, messages, or images you receive. Remember, they may not come through the conscious mind; they can also come other ways. Let go of the need to control and learn to trust.

Learn to discern the difference between true messages from soul and chaotic thoughts. Learn to get clear so that when messages from soul come through, you can hear them more clearly without the mind chatter from the day's events. Learn when to act and when to pull back.

Keep a journal of the things that come through. With the first few attempts at this, just observe. Notice what events occur and the direction you are being led.

Spend a few minutes (fifteen to twenty minutes or even longer) each day doing this. Be patient with the process. The first few times you'll want to spend longer with this exercise to develop the connection. With practice, after a few weeks you'll find you can go deeper more quickly.

To strengthen your mediations, add gemstones to this exercise. Gently hold them in the palms of your hands or place them on your body during this exercise.

Gemstones have different properties and are conductors of energy. Wearing them for a specific task reminds the mind of why you are wearing them. Gemstones can also help you open vibrational doorways to the higher realms. Remember, in order to connect with the higher realms, you must be grounded. Gemstones are both grounding and energy conductors. Charge your stones in a window sill in sunshine or under the light of a full moon, or place them on a piece of selenite to clear other people's energies from your gemstones when you first get them, and to strengthen their abilities.

A few commonly known and readily available gemstones for enhancing soul work include:

1. Amethyst quartz: opens third eye and crown; enhances intuition

2. Labradorite: allows for past life recall; grounds spiritual energy; opens intuition to hidden truths

3. Charoite: accesses and uncovers past lives; links the heart and the crown to the cosmic realms

4. Lapis lazuli: awakens inner vision; aids in past life recall

5. Clear quartz: opens clear connection for soul work; assists with spiritual awakening; clarifies and amplifies intentions

6. Rose quartz: opens the heart connection to the higher realms; releases anger and negative emotions; promotes forgiveness and self-love

chapter 12

Life Preplanning and Manifesting

Allen has experienced a session with me prior to today to get an understanding of what is drawing him to work as a healer. Today is another opportunity to find insight into that, as well as into any residual beliefs that are holding him back in his current life. He wants to explore his relationships with others and gain clarity on moving forward.

On the day of his SESR session, Allen easily moves through time on the way to the spirit world. He stops in the womb, observing his parents at the moment of his conception. He speaks of timing. He knows he is to be their baby and when he's supposed to go in. He zooms right into the fetus, stating proudly that these are the two people he is to incarnate with.

In the womb he has the flexibility to return to the spirit world to go over everything with his guides in preparation for his impending incarnation. For a brief period, he begins to have second thoughts about incarnating. His mother has had two stillbirths after his older brother and he can sense her nervousness over this pregnancy. His father means well but doesn't offer much emotional support, which adds to her stress in knowing that her health is not good and that this is her last chance to have a child.

Allen's guides encourage him to go back and work it out, so he takes the opportunity to do so. This time he "stays" in the developing body to get acclimated for the life to come. The souls of the two stillborn babies stay with him during this gestation period. He can feel their supportive words, as if they're saying, "You can do it." One a girl and one a boy, they know they will not be born. Neither of them has incarnated before. This has been a chance for them to experience a body briefly. The male briefly experiences negativity from the parents' fears and from an older brother, who is used to having his parents to himself.

Being a sensitive soul, Allen notices energy in the womb too. Like when his mother cries, he feels a rush of emotion that causes his own mind to race. He discovers how the emotions motivate the mind and can push it in some directions, so you can feel good or bad.

From here, Allen goes directly into the spirit world through a big light surrounding a wooden door with a brass doorknob. It grows dark as a robed male figure stands holding a scroll. His eyes not seeming friendly, the robed figure motions to Allen to open the scroll. The message inside is "You are here to play." At that moment others jump out and shout, "Surprise, wake up, it's a dream!" It suddenly becomes bright and sunny. He intuitively understands that the message is the world can be dark and light, or lonely and scary … or it can be bright with people who love you. It's all how you dream it so it's up to you.

A screen appears, showing Allen a lifetime where he had experienced things as dark. It was 1927 in Cleveland, Ohio. His name was Henry. He was walking down a city street carrying a briefcase; he was going back to work following a marriage counseling session. Henry was determined to be positive about things and didn't want to lose his marriage.

Henry was a banker and worried about the economy. A lot of people were losing jobs and businesses weren't making enough. People were predicting a depression. It was his job as a banker to get money to help people but a lot of them just weren't good risks for lending money to. Some were even contemplating suicide if they didn't get the loans they needed.

When the Great Depression hit in 1929, Henry lost his job. His wife still had her job as a telephone operator, but it wasn't enough for their family of four. Although he found work in the trades, he could no longer afford his counseling sessions. Eventually, the stress, worry, and fighting got out of hand, and his wife left him to go live with her parents.

Feeling sad and alone, Henry drank a lot. Hanging out at the bars became his refuge. Over time the stress of all of this had an impact on his health. When standing in food lines became too much for him and he was already in bad shape from drinking, Henry committed suicide by putting a shotgun to his head.

At the moment of death, Henry's last thought is that he has made a mistake and is worried he is going to hell. Instead, he finds himself being guided to a place of light in the spirit realm. He is greeted by loved ones who tell him they love him and explain he has a condition that causes him to be depressed. It isn't severe, but the drinking has made it worse.

His guide gently reminds him that prior to incarnating as Henry, he chose to experience suicide. And although he understandably feels guilty about leaving his wife in that way, she is learning too from her side of things. The kids also have their experiences of what it is like to grow up without a father. It is all planned. His guide tells him that each person involved experiences what is needed for their soul's growth. For Henry it has been the experience of feeling completely hopeless and detached, but that it is important now not to hold on to those feelings anymore.

Allen notices that his guide appears as an older Chinese man, who is smiling and wearing a robe like a monk. His eyes now seemed friendlier than before. He is Chinese but following a Tibetan path. He appears this way to remind Allen to have more of this lightness in his life. Allen's guide moves in front of him and sends an energy download to him as he smiles and bows telling Allen he is a "good man." He reassures Allen he will be there to help him develop lightness, giving the analogy of planting seeds, to build upon the positivity and playfulness Allen already has. Moving forward, this will help him with his mission and his spirituality so he doesn't worry so much.

His guide then leads him to a river, the river of his life. Allen is told he must learn to go with the flow more. This will make it much easier on him and the others around him. He and his guide follow the flow of the river. To Allen's surprise, the river spirals uphill, yet it somehow continues to flow. Here, they come upon a small wooded area where it levels out. Allen recognizes this as a place he has been to before. They enter a building called the Building of Judgment.

Inside the building, Archangel Michael is waiting for Allen with an angel on each side. Clients are sometimes greeted by Archangels who provide them with support for their lessons in addition to their own personal guide. Archangel Michael is formal but reassuring as he shows Allen glimpses of planning out the life of Henry with the souls who would have roles as his wife and two children. He shows the scene where Henry is asked if he is willing to do this experiment. It is a gentle reminder for him not to take leaving them this way personally, because all the souls involved will each learn through the experience. This experience has taught him how environment, cultures, and events can affect a soul once incarnate, and even make it more difficult for them.

Archangel Michael tells Allen not to carry those dark feelings, but to live in the light. Henry's family are all there, thanking him for what he has done. He thanks them too for incarnating with him during such a difficult lifetime and for having the courage it took going into that life. Archangel Michael explains that this scene is to give Allen closure on the piece that is holding him back in his current life: he has been feeling unnecessarily responsible for them now, although they are not his family this time around.

The other lesson Henry learns is to see the effect of how people react to money. People put importance on money as being positive or negative, when it's actually neutral. It can be used for good or ill and has effects depending on how it's used, and the value culture puts on it.

As his guide takes him to the "current life planning" to go over his upcoming plans regarding writing and the healing work he will do with others, he tells Allen that he's been on the path for eons and he's going in the right direction. He has the right intentions and is told to not be so hard on himself. More progress can be made with a gentler grasp, and he is reminded that he has a natural love of harmony that's built into his spirit.

Allen's guide tells him that his future is bright—and longer than he thinks. "You don't really understand how much you can manifest if you'll only try to," he advises Allen. "The future is malleable and can be impressed upon." He instructs him to "just think about what you want specifically that will help you grow as a spirit. That's part of spirit; spirit can manifest. We manifest for the greatest benefit of all." Lastly, he reminds Allen not to be shy, but to be clear when asking for help and more fun-loving, too. He adds that you honor yourself as a spirit and human being when you make your needs known.

"Learning the process of manifesting teaches us about the nature of ourselves as humans," his guide informs him. "We are given the ability to form intentions and we have emotions that can help inflame or ignite the intentions. Just like plants need fire (sun), water, air, and earth; we manifest using the same principles as growing seeds and require constant care. Making all our resources available—all of the elements that can be nutritious."

His guide goes on to explain, "Water is also like emotions and water is like consciousness. Every cell has consciousness. In everything that is created there is a flow of consciousness that knows the needs of that plant, animal, or whatever we are trying to manifest. It's like an organism." Everything has consciousness and needs nourishment. And everything we are trying to manifest is like an organism that needs water and nourishment. Emotions are like gut-level inspiration and consciousness that gets imparted to that vision too, so it becomes like a living being manifesting into materiality. The ethereal and psychic dimension are also involved. Allen is encouraged to keep with it and use his wholeness, all of the elements, to manifest. The session ends here.

As a result of the session, Allen feels lighter, having let go of the concerns he had carried from the life as Henry, and with deeper insight into relationships in his life. He is practicing going with the flow more in relationships and in life. He is left with a clearer understanding of how manifesting works and he is excited about how he will take that forward into the healing work he does.

—— *Soul-Minded Exercise* ——
Visualization for Manifesting

You can develop and hone your own skills at manifesting by learning to incorporate these principles. Everything you have now is a result of what you have manifested, the "good" and the "bad." What would you like to manifest or have more of in your life?

1. You can get better at manifesting more of what you desire by getting clear on what you ask for.

2. Observe your thinking and begin to correct yourself when you hear yourself thinking in a negative way. Redirect your thoughts to be more positive.

3. Focus on what you want to create, instead of what you don't want in your life. For example, saying, "*I don't want* to have all of these bills," is not the same as saying "*I want* to be debt free." Or "*I don't want* a partner who cheats" is not the same as "*I want* a partner who is faithful, loving, and appreciates me."

4. How do you feel about what you want to create? Do you feel happy and excited or worried and afraid? Does it lift your energy when you think about having the object of your desire or does it lower your energy? Does what you're asking for feel like you're settling for less

than you deserve? Explore your feelings to identify if what you want to create suits you. Choose those things and relationships that raise your energy and light you up inside.

Sit quietly, free of distractions, and consider what you would like to manifest or have more of in your life. Focus on what you want, not what you don't want. Get clear on what you want. How do you "feel" about what you want to create? Do you believe it is possible? What steps will you need to take to make it happen?

As you envision this, notice how you "feel" about it. Are you excited, happy, or passionate about it? Bring these positive emotions into the vision to nourish your desires into being. Like water nourishing a seedling into maturity, use your emotions and all of your senses (how it looks, feels, sounds, smells, and tastes) to nourish your vision into reality.

Then merge with this vision and allow it to be impressed upon you.

Repeat this often. See it! Feel it! Now be it!

chapter 13
Communicating with Your Guides

Jim is curious about developing his awareness and wants to perceive communications from his spirit guide more clearly during meditations. He wants to create a closer friendship with his guide in a healthy, balanced manner, and to get a clearer understanding of his purpose.

Jim's guide takes him through a series of lifetimes to give insight into the theme of lessons he is working on and what his next theme will be. He is used to order and comfortable following a chain of command due to his military background, which involved working with young recruits in situations designed to push them beyond their comfort zone.

As the All Lives Session began, Jim drifted through time, coming upon an ornately carved door with brass fixtures that opened to a scene in the European countryside. He saw himself wearing leather shoes and pants with a quilted shirt and vest on top. He had on a simple-looking, pointed leather cap, and he had calloused, dirty hands from working as a laborer known as Garin.

It was a pleasant day and the weather was mild on the hillside surrounded by rolling hills, woods, grassland, and cultivated fields on all sides. Garin carried his pitchfork in his hand as he walked along a pathway that had been made along the fence line. He was completely occupied with the task of taking the loose hay from the field and pitching it together so that it could be gathered up into sheaves.

The path came out to the road that ran along the field. Garin and another man loaded the hay into a big cart with wooden wheels. The two men pushed the cart along. After moving it to the next spot, they added more hay and continued this way down the fence line. Jim couldn't help but notice that Garin had "a profound lack of curiosity...he's not a deep thinker," Jim said.

At the end of the day they went home, following a narrow road that led to the village down below. On the far corner of the village across from a stone wall was a row of little round houses with thatched roofs and eaves hanging over them. Outside the doorway of the place where Garin lived hung a bucket that he took down and flipped over to sit on in the shade under the eave. Garin was satisfied to sit in the shade and do nothing. Somehow, he wasn't worried about the future.

Jim is taken by Garin's simplistic outlook. There's a peacefulness about him in spite of having "a profound disregard or concern for anything in the future, ANYTHING! He barely has a conception of eating, which will be in a few hours. It's impossible for him to consider tomorrow, which is far into the future," Jim said in disbelief. In fact, Garin's next meal was too far away to concern himself with yet.

Garin may have been simpleminded, but that didn't seem to matter because he got along well enough this way. He lived on the edge of the village in a room with its own door on the back side of a round stone hut. It was quiet here, which he preferred. His room was furnished with a simple rope bed made of a wooden frame filled with hay just wide enough for one person to sleep. He didn't have a blanket; instead he covered himself in straw to stay warm when it got cold. This worked just fine for him.

When it was time for bed, Garin slept in his clothes. He took off his shoes and put on a pair of socks someone had made for him to keep his feet warm. He liked the feeling of lying on his bed at night when he was tired at the end of the day. He eventually dozed off and slept peacefully.

Each day Garin got up and did whatever people in the village needed him to do. In return, they fed him and looked after him. He was content, and the villagers accepted him this way. No one was mean or cruel to him. If someone needed a hand, he did whatever they needed. He didn't have a close connection to other people, but he wasn't lonely either. He really had no emotional depth. He spent his day carrying stuff and raking stuff and that was enough for him.

It wasn't a complicated life. He just showed up when he smelled food cooking and people fed him. They didn't mind; to them it was normal. Every once in a while, he went to the river to get cleaned up. By the time he did this, he was filthy with dirt. There was no soap. He simply took off his hat and washed his hands and face in the river, rinsing off as much dirt as he could.

As we moved along the life, this was it. No concern for the future or for money. Garin just did what odd jobs came his way, content to accept a meal as payment. He died at thirty years old: tired, gray, starving, and cold.

His spirit peacefully floats out of the body to where his guide greets him on the other side. His guide appears wearing white flowy robes with a mist coming off them. After a few moments of rest and rejuvenation, his spirit feels more like itself, having lifted the density of Garin off of it.

For Soul Reflection, he is led to an empty amphitheater with a fountain flowing like a waterfall. There is an object stuck in the middle of the fountain and everything flows around it. Feeling a little frustrated trying to understand what this means, Jim asks his guide, "Why can't you just pull out a big whiteboard and make it simple?" He intuitively understands this is symbolic of Garin's life, where he was the object stuck in the middle and life just flowed around him. His life lesson is about being in the present moment with absolute absence of future concern. Garin was content living this way. There was no joy, but there was no absence of joy either.

It is initially a bit uncomfortable for Jim's soul to adjust to the absence of curiosity that Garin experiences. This is an example of a life in opposition to one's soul's nature, and in direct contrast to the life that Jim lives now. "Like black and white," Jim says, amused by this. "I was the village idiot."

The session ends with his past life self as Garin sharing a message with his current life self as Jim: "Appreciate the contentment of the moment, like socks on your feet for sleeping in." As Jim leaves my office, this gives him pause to reflect on his own life, a life of order and well-thought-out plans for the future. "There is something admirable, almost, about being content with no thought beyond the current moment," he says as he leaves.

On the drive over for another All Lives Session, Jim finds himself having a disagreement with his guide in the car. Although Jim can't hear his guide, he knows that he is there and questions his guide's qualifications to work with him. He asks to speak to his guide's "supervisor" in our upcoming session so he can get a more competent guide to work with. Jim doesn't tell me this until after the session, but it's important that I point it out here.

The goal of today's session is to continue strengthening Jim's connection to his spiritual team. We discover another lifetime as Jim slips through a spirit door disguised as an elevator door that opens on the other side into a life as a retired schoolteacher named Adele. Adele was an elderly Caucasian lady dressed in a simple floral print dress and sitting in a wheelchair on the porch of the retirement home run by the Episcopal Church. It was 1920 in America in the Deep South.

Adele hadn't always been confined to a wheelchair; she used to be mobile and walk just fine. During her lifetime the automobile was invented and it was becoming popular as an everyday mode of transportation. It's ironic that this is how she came to be in the wheelchair. There was an accident with mixed traffic of automobiles and horses on the street at the same time. Adele was a pedestrian who got caught between a wall and a wagon when a horse got spooked. She was injured as it ran away.

Over the years, Adele became adept at maneuvering the wheelchair with her arms. At first, she disliked the daily routine without the use of her legs, but she adjusted to it. Her injuries had accelerated her retirement and left her confined to the home nearing the end of her life.

Whether it was snapping beans, prepping vegetables for soup, whisking a bowl of something, or wiping off the silverware, Adele continued to be active, helping out where she could. She enjoyed the time prepping food with Ida, the African American woman with the plumpish figure who cooked for them. Adele considered her to be a comfortable friend, whom Jim recognized as someone also in his current life.

Adele was pleased with the life that she led. She was a well-respected high school teacher, proud of herself for being strict to keep the young adults in line. She had never married or had children. She didn't have any family anymore, but the folks at the home were close with each other and got along well. When Adele wasn't helping prepare food, she read the newspaper and books to them.

Adele was seventy-nine years old when she died. The doctor was at her bedside with his black bag, but there was nothing else he could do for her. She wasn't in pain, she was done. Her last thoughts as she died were "Ahh!"

Adele's spirit lingers for a moment before passing into the spiritual realms, and is greeted by the same guide as before. This time he is dressed in business attire: trench coat, hat, and slacks, like a businessman going for a stroll. He takes Jim for a walk in the park, stopping at a bench where they have a seat. He tells Jim that he is dressed this way to appease him in response to his request in the car ride over to "speak to his supervisor" after doubting his capability. "I'm happy to do it ... keep it professional," his guide says. Jim is warmed by this gesture and recognizes there is already a close friendship between them. "If there wasn't a level of trust there, I would never have been as direct with him as I was," he says.

Jim asks how he can be of service to others in a more fun way. His guide responds by pulling out a big whiteboard with a big flower blooming from bud to bloom and places it between them. Jim laughs, recalling that in their last visit reviewing a lifetime, he had asked in frustration, "Why can't you just pull out a big whiteboard and make it simple?" His guide doesn't miss a thing! Jim intuitively understands that the deeper message is if a flower blooms, bees and people will come to it. People will enjoy the aesthetics of it, which occurs naturally. He's to just allow it to happen and enjoy it.

He also understands that the purpose of Adele's life was to develop teaching skills. Her special gift was her clarity of mind and it is because of Adele that Jim naturally knows how to teach. Jim sees Adele waving her hands in the air like a conductor as his guide shares that Adele was best at orchestrating things and people. She gained valuable experience orchestrating PTA meetings, the parents, principals, and the school boards and she was good at it.

Adele had a good understanding of people. She also had an absence of idealism that allowed her not to be bitter. This lifetime helps Jim with a piece he is missing. His guide is extremely pleased with the effectiveness of that life in helping Jim to learn balance, and tells him he needs idealism but in a balanced way.

Adele gives encouragement to Jim regarding having a closer relationship with his guide. She slaps a ruler on the palm of her hand and says, "Don't let up," like she is lecturing one of her students. Jim's guide hugs him enthusiastically, pleased at the prospect. "Having a bonded relationship with the person they're guiding is highly aspirational among guides," Jim muses. The session ends here.

On the day of Jim's SESR session, he is excited about what he will discover. We speak briefly about the other two sessions from the past couple of weeks before beginning the session. Today, Jim's spirit door is a commercial door with a single metal handle, like a submarine hatch. He pushes it open and goes into a nautical scene. It was a foggy night out on the seas as the sub cut through the fog and over the ocean waves lit by the ambient light of the moon. He was an experienced captain commandeering a German naval supply submarine. The sub could go underwater when needed, but it was mostly driven above water like a ship. Only in extreme conditions was it necessary to dive.

The captain moved about the sub in a state of high alertness, as if waiting for something to happen. It was World War I in the waters of the northern Atlantic Ocean. There was always some level of alert because it was wartime. It was the nature of the vessel to go to a location and wait. He never knew if a sub would meet up with them or not. His instructions were to go to the designated point, sit, and wait. The foggy, rainy weather that had rolled in offered security, and allowed them to hide in it.

Captain von Bueling was competent at his job. For him, it wasn't about war or winning; he was just trying to do what he was trained to do. Before the war he had been a ship captain and if there were no war, he'd still be one. It was a normal life and then war happened, and he found himself at sea for the navy. Being a native of Austria had insulated him from politics, not thinking of himself as being on either side; he possessed a strong knowledge of war based on experience. He accepted that his vessel would probably get sunk at some point. It was inevitable; the odds of *not* getting sunk were zero.

Suddenly there was frenetic activity: manually manipulating the dials, spinning them, and closing hatches to keep things secure. Everyone was moving quickly and purposefully. "Dive! Dive! Dive!" was the command Captain von Bueling gave as he threw on his long oilskin coat that hit around mid-calf.

The sub went into its descent, causing the floor to slant. The captain knew they wouldn't make it; something wasn't right. They were hit by explosives from another submarine that punctured the front third portion of their sub. Water began rushing in. Captain von Bueling and his men did what they could, but it was of no use. The infiltrating waters brought the angle of the deck to where it was vertical now.

There was no point trying to get away and there was nowhere to get away to. The captain accepted what everyone on the sub already knew. In fact, this was the reason that the crew members didn't connect with one another on an emotional level. There was only one way it would all eventually end. They worked together to accomplish their job, but there was no sense suffering the heartache of connecting with one another.

The captain stayed with his crew until the final moments, when he confined himself in an isolated area in preparation for the waters to hit. As the waters came seeping in, he drowned. His spirit rose up, leaving his body, observing the scene from above the water littered with bodies and the sub's debris. Captain von Bueling's last thoughts of his life were "Oh, well, that's the end of that."

A guiding force pulls the captain's spirit toward a transparent light where he immediately begins to feel lighter. He is greeted by a friend who takes him through an eye-shaped passageway. On the front side it is earthish, with palm trees and sand; on the other side an astounding light and a permeating sense of purity fill the air. The light comes out and envelops him like an incubator that is safe and healing. Jim reveals, "It's like a conversion, like a retrograde, an undoing like you're a baby. The submarine experience was adrenaline-packed at the end. This incubator is to release that." A bluish-purple light restores an area near his heart that is dark and in need of extensive repair.

Next, Jim sees himself as a bluish figure with a human shape—similar to an Oscar statue, but blue—standing in the center of an oval space. Others like him are positioned around the oval. The space is open and misty in the middle with one side higher than the rest. Five Wise Beings sit on the higher part; one is holding a gold swirl-patterned robe. Jim is captivated by the being with the gold robe and speechless when he discovers the robe is for him. He puts the robe on with a great feeling of accomplishment describing this feeling as "beyond emotion."

As he inspects the robe, he sees that the incredible pattern is made up of blues and greens, and is predominantly gold. It's revealed that he can wrap himself in it and turn into anything. Whatever he turns into is then golden. His imagination takes him through the possibilities of far-out ideas, like a crazy bird dragon creature. These feelings are new for Jim as he revels in it. He folds it in and out of himself, bending, swirling, and flowing with the newness of it all. The Wise Beings delight in Jim's enjoyment of his new gift of creativity, just as they have in watching his growth.

Once playtime is over, things become more solid. The mist clears from the center of the oval space and becomes a big reflecting mirror that turns and rises to face Jim. He pushes into its elasticity and through it to the other side onto a dark, dusty road in a fantastical landscape he likens to the surface of the moon. "It's not something that is, but something that could be created...not bad for my first try," he says. It's a diorama, a representative of a larger story, that holds a naive, idealistic, and childlike scene with a castle, rainbow clouds, and lollipop trees. Lyrics to a song come into his mind carrying the message to go and create.

Next Jim is handed a package to open, with a mirror inside. As he peers into the mirror, he's told, "It's up to me to grade how I'm doing..." He pauses and replies, "I don't feel I've missed many opportunities...and I've been open to the opportunities that have come my way." His guide gives him a whiteboard with a flower blossoming and tells him that his purpose will be achieved if he just does what he is doing now.

The Wise Beings have been helping Jim with the lessons in authority for his last fifteen incarnations. They reveal there is learning in either accepting authority, or by wielding it; whether a navy captain, a school teacher, or even the village idiot. Jim is finishing up the theme of authority now. The next lesson—creativity—has already started with the gift of the robe. He's advised it will be slow going in the beginning while learning about creativity. The gift of discernment learned in other lifetimes will benefit him now.

Upon further Soul Reflection, Jim recognizes that the life as the navy captain was about being comfortable with authority. As captain on a vessel, you're in a position of authority every moment of every day. It becomes part of you. In that lifetime he learned that he didn't have to lean on his authority, he just had to be comfortable being captain and having authority. His favorite thing about that life was the beauty of the openness out at sea, with no light except for the stars in the sky.

On final reflection, Jim smiles, sharing that his guide has been with him through the entire session whether speaking directly to him or not. Jim can see that they were in communication with one another during the quiet times as Captain von Bueling. "Now it's a matter of quieting myself," he says. "We've been communicating better than I think and … it will continue to grow from here."

Jim's guide reminds him to keep meditating to quiet the mind now that our sessions together have helped open up the link between them. Jim laughs, recalling the time when he started this journey into spiritual awareness with an attitude of "let me speak to your supervisor" when he didn't like the answers his guide first gave. He says that his guide's biggest help to him is with reminding him to lighten up and not be so serious. "I'm getting better," Jim muses.

—— *Soul-Minded Journaling* ——
Developing the Habit of Discerning

How do you improve your relationship with your soul? Your guide? Your spiritual team? Start by developing discernment in communicating with your guide.

You can do this exercise wherever you are; just find a quiet space for yourself and bring a journal and a pen. If you can, find an open spot outside with an expansive view, like under the stars at night or from a mountaintop. Feel the vastness opening you to communications from within.

Sit quietly and ponder a question or topic that's on your mind. Choose just one item to focus on.

Listen as your intuition gives you answers. Be patient with yourself. Intuition is your soul's way of speaking to you. Journal these responses. At first, don't act on them yet, just observe while you develop a habit of discerning. Practice stepping back from the conscious mind, letting answers flow through you and not from you (or your mind).

Spiritual messages are softer, like a gentle nudging, not forceful like mind chatter can be. Learn to distinguish between conscious mind and soul mind responses. Learn when to listen and when it's mind chatter. When conscious mind comes in, take a deep breath, and as you exhale, allow it to step back as an observer in the background. When chatter comes in, exhale and let it go like a breath of air being released.

After the end of each week/month, review these answers and notice where there's consistency in the responses. After developing this skill you'll recognize gentle guidance in the messages that come through.

Continue to journal what you discover as you develop a regular practice of this. Over time, notice who is speaking through you (your soul or a guide). If you're not sure, ask and observe the response.

Let these communications become natural to you, strengthening your communications with your spiritual side.

chapter 14
Soul Groups and
Parallel Lives

I enjoy working with twins and have worked with many over the course of my career. I think it gives a great perspective on agreements between souls and how twins incarnate at the same time, each with their own separate purposes. In this story, Elsa and Natalie are twins and Elsa's close friend, Jon, has a special connection with them both.

Meeting Elsa, what strikes me is her authenticity. Elsa is a young woman with a youthful spirit, yet a strong sense of maturity about her. An old soul in a young body, I thought. In pretalk she reveals that she and her twin sister, Natalie, were separated as young girls when their parents divorced, and each parent took custody of a twin. It was a difficult time for everyone, and times of upheaval at home were made worse by not having the other twin around to lean on. When they were old enough to move out on their own, the twins became roommates to make up for lost time.

Elsa's optimistic outlook toward life despite childhood struggles helped her find the courage to start a successful business early on. She fills me in on her unsettled childhood without complaint, simply providing information she feels will be helpful for the session.

Elsa wants an All Lives Session to find out the past lives she, Natalie, and her close friend Jon have all shared with one another, for deeper understanding of others she is cosmically connected to. She seeks reassurances that she has done the right thing, picking up everything to start a new life in an unknown yet somehow familiar place. She admits feeling drawn to her new home even before moving there, and felt a natural kinship with Jon immediately upon meeting him.

As the session begins, Elsa moves to a time in the womb only moments before the twins' birth. Elsa notices her body is a comfortable fit for her soul to inhabit. It is cramped there, and she feels pressure on her chest. The twins don't want to be separated and both want to get out of the womb at the same time. Elsa knows she is supposed to go first, but Natalie is in front, so she tries to maneuver into place ahead of her. Elsa feels lucky and happy about incarnating again, knowing she is here to offer a different approach to the world by her unique perspective.

Next she moves into a past life where she stood outside on a porch dressed in a blouse and a long skirt like clothing worn in the 1930s. Her name was Gracie and she was in her late twenties with long strawberry blonde hair tucked under a large hat. She was holding a little red-headed baby named Anna, nervously waiting and looking for a car to pull up from the direction of the long, dusty, dirt driveway that stretched out in front of the house.

Anna was not Gracie's baby; she was her sister Mary's child. Mary was leaving her abusive husband who kept her in "golden handcuffs." He knew she wanted to get out, so he made every attempt to make it difficult for her to leave. An old red car with a black top pulled up and Mary got out of it. With the baby safe with Gracie, Mary could get away from him this time.

The scene changed to a white schoolhouse in Savannah, Georgia, where Gracie now taught young children their numbers and ABCs. She liked it here so much that she didn't mind the intensity of the summer heat. Gracie, Mary, and Anna [current life twin sister Natalie] had fallen into a comfortable routine in the short time since moving there.

At the school, Gracie was surrounded by children whose little faces she adored. Gracie kept a picture of herself with the man she loved. She longed to be married and have children of her own. A few days ago, Gracie had taken in one of her students into her home. She knew she'd get in trouble for interfering, but she just couldn't help it. She was beside herself watching the boy come to school bruised up by his father. She desperately wanted to save him and although she knew she couldn't, she felt she had to try.

Time elapsed and Gracie, now thirty years old, stood in her kitchen cooking while signing to Anna about something as she ate. She had taught Anna sign language to be able to communicate with her when Mary wasn't there. They had moved again, this time to South Carolina after Gracie was fired from the school for interfering with the mistreated boy. Gracie was married now to the man in the picture [current life close friend Jon] and had a ten-year-old stepson. She and her husband both taught sign language to children at the school for the deaf.

Gracie, partially hearing impaired herself, enjoyed work-ing with the children here even more than at the other school. Most of the children were hearing impaired and had lost their parents for one reason or another. She taught them to over-come their hearing challenges by learning sign language to communicate with their hands. Finding them a new home was also part of her job.

Next, I direct Elsa to move to the next significant time in Gracie's life, but she swiftly moved to a life in Prague during wartime as a school teacher named Anne Wolanski. Anne was only twenty-five years old, living a parallel life around the same time as Gracie's life in the United States halfway around the world, so her soul was living two separate lives at once.

Experienced souls will plan to experience parallel lives when working on particular lessons with their soul group. A great deal of energy is required to do this, so this is not done of-ten or by inexperienced souls. Souls experiencing parallel lives, also known as dual lives, generally incarnate in two different parts of the world to experience different perspectives on cer-tain lessons. The souls' two lives often overlap; while one life is winding down, the other one may be starting. The soul does not meet its parallel self in human form. All three of these souls involved—Elsa, Jon, and Natalie—learn from the experience of living dual lives.

Anne was responsible for the lives of fifteen Jewish children who depended on her to keep them safe. She kept them hidden in her attic to prevent them from being discovered by the mili-tary that occupied Prague. Their Jewish parents had entrusted her with them before they themselves were taken away.

As an Orthodox Christian, Anne didn't believe in the war. She had been living this way for a year now and didn't sleep much at night due to the worry she felt for the children's safety and the fear of being caught. She told the children it would be okay and prayed she could make it until the end of the war, because everyone was counting on her. She felt sad knowing anyone would ever consider hurting innocent children.

Living this way took all her time. The soldiers occupying the streets just outside her house monitored her coming and going. She could only bring in small amounts of food from the market at a time or the soldiers would suspect she was feeding more than herself. They often flirted with her when she walked by. It was a careful dance of being polite to them but not more than that.

One soldier cornered Anne on the street whenever she tried to walk by and wouldn't allow her to pass without talking with him. She found him revolting, but she couldn't risk raising his suspicions, so she played nice to keep the children safe. What disgusted her most was his hatred of people simply because of their religion and the color of their skin. She didn't want to engage with him, but he noticed her groceries, often teasing with her, "You'll gain weight." She had to deal with him every time she left her house.

The money to care for the children came from Anne's sister [current life twin Natalie] who was a wealthy, famous stage actress. Although her sister lived in London, it wasn't safe for her to travel to Prague because she was known to be dating a Jewish man, so she wired the money to Anne to help take care of the children. Anne longed for a partner of her own, admitting she was a little jealous of her sister's freedom and her life.

Anne lived with the constant worry of being found out. After teaching school, she came home and spent time with the children. With fifteen six-year-olds crammed into a small room, it took some doing to manage them. She couldn't risk letting them all out because the soldier she found revolting often stopped by unexpectedly to check up on her. The children loved Anne and understood the seriousness of the situation.

Anne carefully thought out the details to keep things clean and comfortable for the children upstairs. Each child had a mat to sleep on. She did laundry at night and put it away before morning. To conserve water and laundry powder, Anne wore the same outfit several times. She taught the children sign language, so they could communicate without talking. She had a system in place, but she was afraid to go to school, fearful of someone coming into the house while she was away.

As the life progressed, Anne was now into her thirties. The children had been smuggled out of the attic and placed into homes in other parts of the world. Unfortunately, two of them died because no medical care was available. After the war, Anne's sister gave her enough money to leave Prague and buy a building to start her own school in the US. It was hers to run the way she chose.

That dark time in Anne's life filled her with insecurities, but it was worth the hard times knowing she and her sister had changed many lives forever because of what she had done. She was almost "giddy" with excitement to finally live a normal life and go out on a date with a nice man. She finally had the life she dreamed of after those difficult years!

Moving to the end of the life Anne's spirit crosses into the spirit world and is met by the warmth of her grandmother's love. Her guide joins them, revealing that the lesson in both of her parallel lives is learning that she is what she makes of herself and she's to treat people the way she wants to be treated. He reassures her she is on the right track while advising her that by continuing to work hard and being determined to succeed, she will have the things she desires.

After the session, Elsa has a new understanding of the ways she and her sister are cosmically connected to one another and with Jon. As members of the same soul group, they learn through service to others and to each other. Elsa's intuitive connection is stronger, and she recognizes times when she's listened to it, and how it's kept her (and her sister) safe.

When Elsa returns for her SESR session, she is visibly more self-assured. Elsa returns to learn more about the soul connection between the three of them and her current life path.

As Elsa drifts into trance, she returns to the time in the womb just before the twins are about to be born. She knows she is supposed to be born first. It feels cramped to Elsa. She can feel her sister's heartbeat as the "sack above her with Natalie" impinges on her space.

I guide Elsa to a less confining period and she goes to the seventh month where the twins lie parallel to one another, touching but with room between them. By incarnating as twins, they will rely solely on one another, grateful to have each other to lean on. Where one is weak, the other will provide support, and they will go through some experiences simultaneously. They often incarnate in mother/daughter roles, with Elsa the mother figure. She feels lucky to incarnate with a twin, knowing not many souls get to have one.

Elsa joins the fetus at the second month to be with Natalie, but goes back and forth to the spirit world for final instructions from her guides before permanently settling in. In preparation for the challenges she will face, she chooses a mind and body that are complementary to her soul's essence. The mind is adaptable, appreciative, and open to seeing different points of view. Elsa genuinely wants to help people, and expects nothing in return. "I just want love in my life," she says.

They chose these parents because they wouldn't be the kind of parents to control their children's lives. This allows the twins the freedom to mold their own lives. While it may be difficult not having parental support, it allows them the latitude to be who they choose to be in life.

Whenever Elsa feels her mother's stress, she tries to help by not moving and being still. The twins are also aware whenever they are around smoke and unpleasant smells because it makes them feel itchy, trapped, and claustrophobic. The unpleasant odors scare Natalie, who clings to Elsa for comfort. They communicate by squeezing each other's hands, reassuringly.

Elsa continued to explore her soul connections as she was guided by a bright light to a lifetime in France. Her name was Abigail, Abby for short. Her father was the king. Abby was about twenty-five years old, and was dressed in a long silk dress, with her curly blonde hair pinned up, exposing her very pale skin. She adorned herself with bracelets, rings, and strands of pearls. Her husband was a French general who protected the royal family. They lived at the palace and she also helped with the children.

The general was gone for long periods of time; this time the battlefield was in Asia. Although he was a general, he didn't enjoy the fighting; he had his ambitions set on being king. Once they were married, he spent very little time with Abby, which suited her just fine because she was in love with someone else. She quickly realized he only married her to get close to her royal family, so not to be sent into battle anymore.

Rich tapestries and beautiful paintings embellished the walls of the huge palace. Standing with her bejeweled hand outstretched on an ornate chair, Abby watched over her four younger step-siblings at play and a fifteen-year-old who would be heir. She was responsible for changing them, seeing that they were fed, and playing with them. Her favorite was fourteen-month-old Paden [current life twin Natalie]. Abby didn't mind watching over the children, in fact, she preferred it to the general's company.

Abby reminisced of the time before she married the general, when she mingled with the villagers in the market outside the palace gates and covertly sold trinkets there. She was in love with Paul [current life close friend Jon], one of the merchants. Paul loved her as much as she loved him. He believed in her and encouraged her independence from the royal family. When her father found out, he forced her to marry the general instead, and found her a more suitable job at the palace.

During his twelve-year reign, the king developed a reputation for being an evil king. He abused his power to start unnecessary wars and treated people cruelly, including beating his current wife. When Abby was very young, her mother died, but she knew it wasn't an accident like she had been told. Abby's grandmother, whom she loved and trusted, was queen then. She secretly advised her granddaughter to get out when she could because the government would collapse, and it wouldn't be safe for any of them. The queen passed away shortly after, and Abby's father became king.

Years later, Abby saw her opportunity to escape this life when she witnessed the general kill someone higher up to advance his career. She didn't tell anyone, but instead leveraged this to gain her freedom. The general agreed to help her run away with Paul and not tell anyone so in return he would have a chance to be king.

A plan was launched for Abby and her true love, Paul, to escape to another country to live as commoners. A property and new identities were arranged for them as bakery owners. Abby was happy to trade a life of misery to be with the one she loved. It was made to look like a kidnapping. Paul and Abby took Paden with them knowing he was in danger of being murdered by a king fearful of being replaced by his own heirs.

When the government collapsed, families fought amongst themselves. Fathers fought sons and brothers fought brothers. The general kept his word but died in battle and never became king. After the collapse, it was safe for Paul and Abby to marry. She took Paul's surname and happily relinquished her royal title, declaring, "No money or title in the world is worth not having freedom."

Paul and Abby had a nice life together. They didn't have children of their own, but they were happy they saved Paden's life and raised him as their son. Paden enjoyed baking, playing outside, and fishing with Paul. Abby felt so lucky to have a good life with Paul, who ran the bakery and taught people to cook. She especially enjoyed watching Paul sitting in his chair in the mornings, which gave her "a rush of happiness to see him."

Paden grew up and fulfilled his dream of becoming a doctor. He was with Abby when she died as an old woman in her own bed. Paul passed just a few years before and she knew it was her time to join him. Her spirit is wrapped in light as she is guided home.

Her male guide greets her, moving around her like a breeze "reading" her energy. He ignites a familiar spark Elsa's felt many times before. He reminds her to trust herself more and rely on her "gut instincts" that have saved lives in past and current life situations as he sends balls of purple, white, and yellow light to lessen Elsa's worry. He adds that, although she has saved some-one many times in the past, you can't always save them; the inevitable will happen when it's their time to go.

In Soul Awareness, her soul's feminine energy feels like a warm feeling, "like many souls in one... from the many life-times I've experienced," Elsa shares. Her soul reminds her, "Trust your guides more and be aware you have them... have more faith in mankind too." She's to ask for help and have faith that her guides will provide what she needs, remembering they are here to help her succeed. She shows Elsa how she comes into her mind to assist when she's having a bad day and how the feelings in her stomach are gut instincts kicking in. Elsa is advised to be aware of this and learn about the law of attrac-tion to create what she wants.

Elsa, Natalie, and Jon are part of a soul group that works with energy and healing the mind. There are others in the group but the three of them work very closely together. In the spirit world, their job is to send energy to young souls that strength-ens them for their next lives. When the three of them incarnate, they help others with their touch. Each of them has their way of doing this. Jon's hands heat up when this happens. Elsa's empathic abilities help her recognize when people need help before things spiral out of control. She helps people feel better by listening and by being there.

Elsa's and Natalie's souls are uniquely intertwined to ensure they don't fail to grow. The two of them have shared all of their incarnations together, but this is the first time they've both incarnated as the same age. It's a gift to have a twin to share these experiences simultaneously. This time around they'll en-joy each other as sisters, not as parent and child. As soul mates, Jon and Elsa balance one another and help each other to grow in an adapting way. The two of them work in harmony with each other, making their daily lives easier. They aren't always together. Jon sometimes stays behind and assists from the spirit world while Elsa incarnates with Natalie. Elsa asks about Natalie's soul mate, but is told it's not for her to know, and not to worry, she'll find hers.

During Soul Reflection, Elsa's guide shares glimpses of other relevant lifetimes on Earth, including one where both she and Natalie incarnated in a clan of cavemen. As Elsa observes that life, the smell of raw meat permeates her senses. They survived on nothing. It was all that they had, and they were fine. They shared food—raw red meat and plants—with the others and communicated with their hands, not words. Another lifetime of sign language, but somehow, they all knew what was being said.

Elsa is given a glimpse of a future life and told that someone she loved, who has already passed, left to get ready for their next life together. Next time around, Elsa will be an older sister to Natalie and Jon will be there too.

Elsa's most significant earthly lifetimes are the ones as Anne in World War II, protecting children, and as Abby, learning to provide for herself while recognizing that money is power to be used wisely. Both lifetimes she developed strength of courage that she's finding in her current incarnation. As Abby, she fulfilled her purpose by saving Paden's life and ultimately stopping the king's heirs from perpetuating a government that hurt people. As a doctor, Paden saved lives instead. Abby learned that knowing and being who you are is more important than a title. When something is not right, walk away.

In her current incarnation Elsa will "save people in a less stressful environment than in the other lifetimes and in subtler, more beautiful ways. It will be less stressful than it was in the past, no killing, hate, or anger." She's incarnated to create a new way. What started as an idea is manifesting into much more that will make a difference in the lives of many people. She'll have a partner this time around. It will take some time, but their current jobs are giving them skills they will need. Hard work and focus on her current career will take her to the next one in time.

Next, Elsa is led to a white and gold room to visit with her Soul Advisory Council. She is in the middle of a circle surrounded by Wise Beings wearing white robes. A new guide joins her in the circle while one who has been with her throughout many lifetimes stays in the background. This new guide will help Elsa with moving on to bigger things and letting go. The Wise Beings hug her and tell her how happy they are with her progress and that they are helping her have a happy spirit.

The Wise Beings point out the significance of entering each of the past lives as a young woman is to show her how she chooses lifetimes of adversity that help her to find strength. They tell her not to question her integrity or strength; she's always had it.

Before closing the session, Elsa is told to treasure her new home and the chance to explore a new life. She can connect with her spiritual team for guidance in meditation or quiet moments. To get started she's to "take a minute every day to ask for what I want and believe I'll get it…I'll feel better noticing it when it shows up. Instead of saying, 'I can't,' or 'I don't,' be grateful for what I have and knowing I am loved."

As Elsa emerges, she is happy and relieved to know she is on the right track. Knowing her soul connection to Natalie and Jon gives her comfort. Things seem to fit better knowing what she knows on a deeper level. Her soul's magnificence shifts her insecurities and she feels proud of the life she's making for herself. Seeing Anne overcome the challenges she faced while dreaming of a better life shows her that she can overcome just about anything and have what she wants in life with hard work and focus.

After she shares the past life details with Jon, he says a déjà vu feeling came over him, reminding him of the amazing ways their souls and lives are connected; it helped to explain things he has felt before. It's a gentle reminder that everything we do in life matters. He always knew in his heart that Elsa was his soul mate; it is something he's felt all along.

Who knows where this will take them? Only time will tell. Elsa, Natalie, and Jon have a lot of love in their lives between them and around them. No matter what, they know there is a strong bond between them that keeps them close with one another.

—— *Soul-Minded Journaling* ——
Changing Thoughts from "I Can't" to "I Get To"

Do you find yourself in a loop of worry or fearful thinking? Do you hear yourself saying "I can't"? Although some things are a chore that must be done, changing your attitude can help lighten the burden of the load. What can you let go of that's holding you down?

How about changing that thought process from "I can't" by saying "I get to"? What do you get to do? What would you like to do more often? What are your passions in life and what do you find fun?

Remember your soul and your guides are with you. They hear your requests and want you to succeed. Clearing the fearful thinking helps you to be better in touch with their guidance.

Put your positive mindset into motion: Take a minute every day to ask for what you want and believe you'll get it. Begin to notice when it shows up. Notice over a period of time how you no longer say "I can't," but rather "How can I?" or "I get to."

What do you get to do today?

—— *Soul-Minded Practice* ——
Salt Bath Relaxation to Release Worry

It's difficult to create, bring more joy into your life, or connect with spirit when you're tense from worry and stress. A physical way to rebalance your energy is with salt baths. A cup of sea salt or Epsom salts in a bathtub of water is therapeutic and releases pent up energies in the body's energy field. It's an alternative to salty ocean water when you aren't able to go to the beach. Add a few drops of your favorite essential oils to enhance the experience.

At the end of the day, draw yourself a sea salt bath, put on relaxing music, and unwind while you go over your "I get to" affirmations in your mind.

chapter 15
Reconnecting to Find
Presence and Passion

As a research scientist, it's Madison's job to provide unbiased data upon which conclusions can be drawn. "It isn't my job to draw the conclusions, but rather to provide the basis where it could be drawn. It is not good or bad, it is fact. As scientists, we want to make a positive impact, for the good of society," she tells me.

Madison brings a list of questions with her for the All Lives Session. She is curious about her past lives and has some of the typical questions that people have for these kinds of sessions: What is my purpose for this incarnation? What causes me to feel blocked or exhausted for no particular reason? Why am I especially drawn to Native American cultures and experiences? What past life should I visit that would have the greatest impact/meaning for my present life?

In pretalk, Madison shares that as a child she was drawn to Native American books even before she could read. She immersed herself in anything Native American. Her favorite game was playing "Indians," which for her meant hunting buffalo, searching for food for her family, and making tepees out of rags. As she got a little older, her parents took her to a Cherokee reservation, where she was devastated to see the reality of life there.

As a kid, Madison also enjoyed sitting under a tree meditating to commune with nature. She chose the field of science as a way to work close to nature and try to understand how it all works. She is curious about the spiritual connections humans experience and wants to explore them further. Madison mentions that she had been disillusioned by her religious upbringing, feeling that the idea of prayer feels disingenuous to her now.

As the session begins, Madison lets her awareness turn inward. Moving through time, she recalls an experience when she is very young, standing alone in the driveway at her house. It has just started to rain. She takes delight in feeling the warmth of the concrete under her feet and smelling the fresh scent of the rain. She enjoys how she felt so connected to nature and to everything and not separate from it.

Crossing through the abyss of time, Madison notices a white door surrounded by darkness. Images and sensations begin flooding in as she moves through the spirit door. Her body feels larger than her actual size and her feet are cold as if immersed in a cool stream of water resting along the smooth stones lining a stream bed. Her body feels flattened out as if it is a landscape itself when suddenly the notion of a mountain comes to her. "Am I the landscape or am I a person with my feet in water?" she wonders. It is confusing for her at first with the rush of sensations she is feeling. Is this a past life or something else?

It is around dusk. The weather is warm, like a summer evening. In the distance the rich green of the pine trees stands out against the backdrop of brown from the rocks and boulders. The reflection in the water reveals an older Native American man with long, straight, black hair and "fit feet" that are used to walking. He has dark eyes. He discovered this place while roaming the area and returns here whenever he can.

This special place feels familiar to Madison. "I feel that I've been here before, I enjoy this place ... it's a very sensory place, because the water is so cold, but the rest of me feels pretty warm ..." she says as she bursts out weeping, while waving her arms through the air trying to feel the energy there. "This is a way of being a part of everything. I don't have to worry about anything. I'm not thinking about where I'm going to go. I miss life that was like that!" Madison exclaims with a big sigh. "I have a feeling of gratitude; that I have come here to pray!" For a moment she is taken aback by the idea of praying, but intuitively understands this place is the reason why she has such a strong kinship with Earth. She is thankful for this connection and she doesn't want to see Earth destroyed! Her weeping intensifies as she says this.

We end the session. This is enough for one day. After an intense couple of hours, Madison needs rest, so she can continue with our SESR session the next morning. This session has been filled with many long pauses and big releases through exhalations and tears. Sometimes the most powerful sessions are the ones where fewer details are given, yet more intense energy downloads are felt as the soul recalibrates the client's energy field. What's most important is the connection that's made. I hope that we will be able to pick up here in tomorrow's session, but I also know that sometimes the guides have another plan in mind. We will find out tomorrow.

The next morning, Madison arrives refreshed and ready to go. She's noticeably lighter and comments that she feels as if something that had been hanging over her has been lifted. We begin the SESR session and almost immediately after the induction process, Madison notices darkness and a sensation of hands coming together to clasp in midair as if in prayer. She feels guided to move her hands together that way. Putting her hands together, she realizes that this is the "namaste" greeting of respect. Her guides greet her with this gesture, which in Sanskrit means "the Divine in me honors the Divine in you" or "I bow to the Divine in you." She is deeply moved by this as she reciprocates.

Next, she feels heat releasing in her solar plexus. She senses someone familiar moving in close toward her, hugging her. As she hugs back, they whisper in her ear, causing her to cry. "Why the emotion?" I ask. "I don't know; it's like missing someone," Madison replies. The tears increase as she becomes aware of a light that returns her to the sacred space with the stream and the rocks where we had left off the day before. She feels the rocks under her feet and hears the "whooshing" sound of the rushing water. Fireflies with orange sparks of light flash against a backdrop of the pine trees. She weeps more as one gently lands in her hand.

"I feel so connected to them," Madison says in childlike amazement. "I hold these creatures in my hands. I love them so much! The little birds, the feeling of them landing on my head…the little ones, so round and chunky, everything is so alive! It makes me feel joyful! I don't talk to them, I just know them. I just hang out with them," she laughs. She begins to feel a little shaky as she continues to release heat from deep within her belly, solar plexus, and psoas muscle.

Madison lets out a big sigh as she realizes this scene of the stream cutting through the mountains resembles something that she's painted since she was a teenager. It appears as an open space, like a gate split by mountains on each side. The open space with the crack through the earth allows a spirit to come through the opening. When she paints it, she often illustrates the scene as a nighttime landscape with a moonlit road going through the desert and the mountains on each side with lush waterfalls. Madison "knows" this place. She has painted it many times before.

A series of deep exhalations follow as her body continues to let go of its pent-up energy. "There is so much releasing. I feel shaky, it's just everywhere. I feel trembly, my back muscles…even my elbows?" she chuckles. She pauses for a long while as these sensations work their way through her. "I feel like I'm inhabiting my body more…like I'm ready to pay attention…I'm feeling very calm now…like my mind is trying to experience the still point [between the two hemispheres]," Madison remarks as she points to the middle of her forehead.

The energy comes from the center of Madison's body, like blasts of heat that cause her to break out into a sweat. A great sadness comes into her heart like a white-hot heat. It's there momentarily, like a flame, before it immediately changes to something wonderful. She describes it as "feeling heat releasing from my gut! Sweating, like fire and water, it's like *whoosh*!"

I ask Madison's guides to reveal insights to her along with the sensations she feels to interpret what is happening. "I'm not really here…I'm just trying to get through it [life]," Madison replies. "I want to be more present. I had that feeling as a child, as being present, and I feel that at one point, it went away." With each release she is more present in her body.

Everything is becoming clearer. Although I try, Madison's guides bypass the questions she lined up for the session, choosing instead to take her through the spirit door and into this sacred space designed just for her to reconnect and remember. She knows this place is hers to return to whenever she needs, whether in her meditations, her paintings, or her dreams.

After the energy surges, Madison notices that she feels more alive, more empowered, and a little more whole. Even the insides of her teeth are tingling! "I feel like things are going to be okay. I feel okay ... my feeling of passion is coming back," she says as she makes a gesture with her fist over her heart. "My heart is feeling more open. I feel like I have a right to be here as much as anyone else."

I ask Madison to tell me where in her body she feels the energy of "feelings of belonging here just like anyone else." She describes it as "a feeling that is filling up in my body ... a feeling of my feet being planted, a feeling that comes out of the gut ... a feeling of determination, of being focused ... I've felt like I've been scrambling, but now I want to be focused ... liberation can allow one to be focused." She motions with her arm straight out ahead like an arrow flying away from her, stating that this gesture itself helps her with focus.

She sees her body as if looking down on it from above. A white light the color of volcanic fire outlines her stomach, like lava but not hot. Over her midsection, she observes two domes of light: the first is over the sacral chakra and the second is over the solar plexus chakra. It appears like a bright white light with red-orange molten lava spewing around the edges of the white light and cooling. "It's like fire in the belly," she chuckles.

Next come tears of joy: "I'm getting a part of myself back...I'm feeling more integrated. I can be here [Earth] AND not be compromised. I can be here AND do what I need to do. I can be here, AND I can have joy," Madison exclaims. "It's the power of choice, choice is very powerful. You can choose, there's no need to judge. Be free with your love, express the love. It lightens and helps every single person. So much repression! I have so much to offer. I went through a phase in this life where I got really beaten down and crunched up and I feel like this [session] is helping me come back." More heat surges through Madison's lower chakras from the sacral up to the heart chakra.

I try again to get answers to the questions Madison has on her list. I ask about her career and the work that she does. It takes a moment, as if responding requires switching gears in her brain from the physical releases to find the answers to the questions. "My work feels restricted," she replies. "I feel that it's noble work. In this world, people want the numbers, they want to see the numbers, they want to know how bad is this thing, do I need to worry about it? I'm in a place where I can provide the unbiased information...maybe somehow these numbers will make an impact...I sit at a desk all day and I read, and I write, and that feels so restrictive."

I ask, "And so what is your passion?" Madison replies, "I feel passionate about helping people reach their fullest potential...I wanted to be an educator at one point to create a place where children can simply be who they are, find out who they are, and feel the curiosity of exploring this world. Maybe it comes from my own feelings of having been repressed or smashed down; or being closed up or walled off and not knowing about how extraordinary this world is. I would like to bring a flow to help them see how everything is connected."

Madison admits that she knows her guides are in constant communication with her, especially in her dreams, though at first she doesn't always understand the messages they send. "I dreamed about candy for months! I used to have the most horrible nightmares, but then I had a bunch of dreams about spontaneously encountering candy! Life can be sweet, it's okay!" she said. "There can be sweetness, even in this life, which is sooo far away from the [Native American] one. I'm realizing that it all has value, it all has lessons. I just need to be focused."

Next, Madison's guide calls her by her soul name. She joins with her soul's energy and feels it activating a soul recalibration deep within that realigns her with her true self. More big exhalations follow. Her soul's message is for her to not be afraid to express her joy and creativity! "It's my right as a human being to feel like this...to be open!" she happily exclaims.

We briefly explore the connection between her soul, body, and mind to learn whether her soul is in alignment with this mind, or in opposition to her soul's energy. "We [soul/body/mind] are able to work together. We can see both sides [right and left brain] to integrate it. Modern life is so hard. So distracting. This side has to think and think and think and think to get money. There's got to be an easier way," she responds. "So serious...it's time for some fun and finding delight in the world." A white crystal shaped into a half moon is placed in Madison's chest with an arrow covered in feathers coming out of it. It points straight ahead as a reminder to her to not get distracted and keep her focus.

A deeper message about integrating both hemispheres of the brain emerges: "In modern life, all of these brilliant souls who have so much to give are scrambling to live. There are so many important things to do. The world's got to change, each person needs to change, each person makes a choice. The choice comes from their heart, from a very deep place. Everyone knows, deep down inside. The pain comes from them not knowing this. It's knowing. It's just knowing. The left side of the brain has trouble understanding, but it's how we live in this world now. But they can work together."

The session begins winding down. Before emerging with Madison, I thank her guides for allowing me to be part of such an amazing session they've carefully crafted to take her out of her analytical mind and into her emotions to rebalance her chakras. Recreating a sacred place from a past life that has been special to her gives her a place to revisit in the future whenever she needs to recharge or be more connected to the world around her. I finish by asking for a keyword to serve as a reminder of the day's session. The word is "joy."

After the debrief, Madison leaves feeling lifted up and has a great deal to integrate. A few weeks after her session, Madison writes to share that her chakras are still abuzz, and she feels grounded and much more herself. She's more comfortable with life and interested to see what lies ahead. She felt inspired and has since completed training in energy work as the healer in her has been awakened.

—— *Soul-Minded Exercise* ——
Full Moon Meditation

If you feel that you are tired and worn out and have lost your connection, find your connection now. There are many beautiful places in nature for you to sit, unwind, and reconnect. If you especially need a boost, then finding a spot by water or under a full moon can be nice to synchronize your energies with nature. Remember to stay hydrated too. Water helps the emotions in the body to flow.

Sit under the full moon for twenty minutes, gazing up into its light. Bathe in its luminous glow, appreciating the healing properties of connecting with the moon's magnetic forces.

For the first ten minutes, just connect to the moon's energy. Breathe it in as you let go of the distractions and chaos in your mind that affect your ability to "feel" what you feel. With each exhale, release the feelings or thoughts keeping you from having peace of mind or the ability to stay focused and present in your life. Release the pent-up energies and worries keeping you feeling keyed up or affecting your belief in yourself or blocking you from being compassionate with others.

Let it heal old wounds in your heart. If negative emotions come up, let them. Tears are a therapeutic release mechanism designed to help the emotional body release pent up emotions that are blocking your connection.

For the next ten minutes, set your intentions for the coming weeks/month. Use this time to problem-solve or look at a situation from another perspective. Bask in the light of the moon and let the moon's energies shed light on whatever is on your mind. Let the moonlight rekindle your childhood feelings of amazement looking up into the moon. Feel it opening your heart.

Learn to be still as you sit quietly under the full moon. Where are you in your thinking—the past, present, or future? Bring your thoughts into the present. Listen for important messages from your soul.

Each night following the full moon, sit under the moonlight for a few minutes and make this connection stronger as you feel the moon's energies and your connection to it growing. Notice how your load gets lighter and new solutions to old problems come to light. Notice new messages in your mind opening you to intuitive guidance. Ask the moon to light your path to show you a way to move forward in the darkness.

In addition, place your gemstones and jewelry in a windowsill under the light of a full moon to recharge them. Once charged up, wear them to keep this connection open.

chapter 16

In Search of
True Love

Kathy is an intelligent, well-educated career woman who is re-
covering from a serious illness that has caused her to take a
good hard look at her life and begin making changes. She is
missing a true love in her life and is ready for a committed, loving relationship. She hopes that SESR can help her to explore
relationship patterns she has come to recognize, especially
emotionally abusive relationships with men, to understand the
deeper reason for deep-rooted feelings of abandonment she is
left with when these relationships end.

Kathy is curious if there is a pattern of behavior in her past
lives that can further explain this. She is most unsettled by an
affair she previously had with Paul, a married man. She is curious as to whether she's ever been married to Paul in a past life.
Mostly, she is ready to move on from the pain this affair has
caused her.

We learn that Kathy and Paul are karmically entangled in
several of their past lives. Kathy's guide shows her a series of

lifetimes that parallel her painful current life relationship with Paul that has left her questioning why she allowed it. (Note: For clarity, I've kept the names as Paul and Kathy throughout all of these past lives listed below, although they each had different names with each incarnation.)

As the session unfolds, we discover that Kathy and Paul were married and lived in a cottage on the edge of his family's Southern plantation in the early 1800s. Kathy was in her early teens when she married Paul, who was ten years older. They started their family almost immediately when Kathy gave birth to a baby girl. Paul was very unhappy with Kathy for failing him by having a girl, but was overjoyed when not long after she gave him a son.

Unfortunately, their son contracted a high fever from a sickness that was going around, and died when he was only a toddler. Although many people in their town died from this same thing, Paul blamed Kathy for the boy's death and refused to forgive her for it despite the fact that she had unknowingly taken the baby around others who were sick. Kathy blamed herself too. "I was a baby having a baby for him," she said, "but that was a normal thing."

The death of their son fueled Paul's rage toward Kathy for failing him. One day, while she was in the kitchen making biscuits, Paul stormed in complaining about something else she had done wrong. It was not a happy time for them. No matter how hard she tried, it was never good enough for Paul anymore.

Kathy had just suffered a miscarriage and was still healing from it. Her doctor warned her not to get pregnant because her body couldn't handle another pregnancy. Paul knew this but forced himself on her anyway. He was determined to get her pregnant. He told her that if she didn't get pregnant this time, he would leave her.

Kathy was never able to get pregnant again. Paul continued to punish her for not being able to have another son. Sometimes he'd leave for long stretches of time. He told her he was ashamed of her because she couldn't give him the son he desperately wanted. Then he went and had one with someone else. She felt lonely, scared, and abandoned.

Despite the affair, Kathy stayed married to Paul. She looked after their daughter while she waited and waited for him to take her back, but he never forgave her for the death of their son. Most of the time Paul stayed with the other woman and eventually they had a second child. Kathy stayed in their small cottage on the edge of the property and when Paul inherited his family's wealth, he moved his mistress into the big house and lived there with his other family.

Kathy was young and beautiful when they married, but now she was feeble and malnourished. She was barely thirty years old, but the pain and hurt of his betrayal and abandonment weighed heavily on her. She was lonely and depressed, which caused her not to have much of an appetite at all. Most of the people who knew her felt sorry for her, while others put the blame on her for not being able to give Paul another son. Kathy blamed herself too for not being able to get pregnant again after their son died. After years of living this way, Kathy's heart grew weak and her body frail. She lived a lonely existence until she died of a broken heart. They buried the remains of her tiny body there on the plantation.

What a painful life that had been! Kathy knew she didn't want to go through that again. Her guide greets her weary spirit, informing her that unfortunately she is doing it again but in a different way. "Enough is enough. It's time to stop this now. It's time to have joy every day," he says. "No more drama, no more pain, and no more feeling like you're not good enough." Kathy admits Paul made her believe she wasn't good enough. Her guide reminds her that she's changed.

Her guide hugs her, sending waves of healing energy through her to release the pain and heaviness of the life on the plantation. After comforting her, Kathy is guided to Soul Reflection to take a look at another past life with Paul that's important for her to see.

This past life opens to a scene of Kathy being raped by Paul in an alley. In that life, Paul was a politically powerful businessman and Kathy was an attractive, confident young woman from a good family. Paul made several advances toward Kathy, but she rejected him. He wasn't used to being told "no" by a woman, so he decided to take what he wanted to teach her a lesson.

He followed her and dragged her into the alley. Pressing the weight of his body onto her from behind, he pinned her face against the brick wall with her hands behind her back and forcibly raped her. She was half his size and helpless against his physical strength. During this encounter, they were interrupted by a passerby. Upon being found out, Paul immediately threw Kathy to the ground, buttoned his suit trousers, and stormed away.

It took a long time for Kathy to heal from the emotional wounds of the rape. There was no one to turn to about what had happened. Paul was a powerful man who most were afraid to cross. Kathy didn't want news of it to get out either. She knew it would ruin her reputation and hurt her family if it did.

Her physical appearance was altered because of it too. She bore a physical scar on her cheek for the rest of her life, a constant reminder of having her face pressed against the brick wall. This shattered her confidence in herself and was the reason she never married in that lifetime.

Next, Kathy's mother appears. Although she has already crossed over in the current life, she is here to let Kathy know that she is not going through this alone. She is with her in spirit, along with her guides, helping from the other side.

She explains to Kathy that these lifetimes are lessons about power. Sometimes Kathy has the power, but in these lifetimes others had it. She tells her that her current incarnation is about learning not to let others use her or control her because it causes too much pain. She's to learn to find someone who loves her unconditionally. To do this, she must first love herself unconditionally and not allow others into her life who don't.

Kathy's mother informs her that a new love is coming. Her soul mate is on the way now that she's completed the lessons she was meant to learn. She can trust again. Her soul mate won't cheat or abandon her. She adds that he's been learning his own lessons while she's been going through hers. Now it's time for them to find one another. She reassures her daughter that her soul mate will love her "more than you ever thought that you could be loved."

Kathy is advised that she went through all of this to find her true love. She's learned what love is not and she's broken the cycle of behavior. Kathy begins to feel a healing energy pouring into her heart, melting the heartache and distrust she's carried from this cycle of betrayal. Kathy sees a big red heart like the one her mother gave her before she passed.

Her mother says not to worry: now that Kathy "gets it," she won't to let it happen again. Her grandmother joins them. "Finally!" she says. They help Kathy clear out the last threads of the old energy from her illness and tell her it's important that she learn to set boundaries and to say no! She assures Kathy there's no need for more pain or heartache, only love now.

They surround her with a circle of white light and tell her that what's left for her to do is forgive herself. Kathy readily does this. She's carried the shame and guilt from all of this for too long. Kathy shrinks the red heart symbol and places it in her heart for strength.

With the help of her guide, Kathy is shown glimpses of future scenes with her new love who will be coming her way once she completes cutting the energetic ties that bind her to Paul. She won't miss it, she'll know, and he will too! They'll be happy together.

They praise Kathy for all the good work she's done to work through these agonizing incarnations with Paul, advising her that this is their last one. Her guide then cuts the final cord that connected Kathy and Paul to one another. As he does this, golden colors like fireworks shoot through her, cleansing her spirit from these lifetimes of pain. Kathy feels her soul expand upon being free from this painful bond with Paul.

Kathy's mother also tells her to stop worrying about being sick; the treatments worked, and her health will continue to improve now that she's learned to take better care of herself. The illness served a purpose and provided her with information she'll use to help others. Everything is falling into place now and she is taking the necessary steps to make it happen.

Kathy is reminded that her soul group's common focus is on lessons of forgiveness. Paul didn't show up in Kathy's soul group, but rather a companion group assisting with these lessons. Although it's been difficult, the pain offers the opportunity to forgive. Kathy is changing the pattern midway through this lifetime. Her guide tells her that things will get better as he reminds her that it may seem like small steps but to have faith and patience; things will turn out okay.

Lifetimes of loneliness and depression take a lot out of a soul. Between these extremely difficult incarnations, Kathy's soul "rests up," building up happiness with her loved ones to prepare her for the next life. Her grandmother adds, "You've already broken the pattern in your current life and the outcome will be different than the other times. It's time for joy now!" Kathy reveals that her grandmother experienced a life of loneliness and pain that ended her life prematurely. Kathy has chosen a different path, breaking the family's pattern, and her own. There are fireworks again, celebrating the new Kathy that has emerged. She is physically and emotionally stronger now, despite the experiences she's been through.

Kathy is led to a big building with Greek architecture and columns lining the front. This building with its strong columns represents this stage of her life as a new beginning. Waiting inside are her Soul Advisory Council, who appear as male figures wearing white robes and sandals, with greenery in their hair. Her guide, a strong male presence, joins them.

Kathy kneels in front of this panel of strong male energy, who are here for support. She's told she needs strong men in her life because she's not had that in her romantic relationships. They show her that strong men can be loving and respect her. It's been a long time coming, they say, but they're proud of the progress being made. Kathy knows she's changed and is proud of herself too!

At the end of this briefing, Kathy is taken to a door that leads her to a beautiful place with greenery, birds, and flowers. The session ends with one door slammed shut and another one opening. Kathy happily walks through the open door into the beautiful, joyful place.

Following the session, Kathy leaves my office with her confidence restored. She feels better with an understanding of the karmic entanglements between her and Paul, and is happy to resolve them. She is excited and optimistic about what the future holds.

A year goes by and Kathy calls me for another session. She is confused and wants clarification. She also hasn't met her soul mate within the time she had expected it would happen. She wants to understand. Has she missed something?

The follow-up SESR session quickly moves to a scene with Kathy running down a long corridor trying to choose which lifetime to explore. A blue door catches her attention, but she is reluctant to go in when she peeks inside and sees Paul.

Paul was her husband and he was not happy with her. In fact, he was angry and yelling at her. His hands were around her neck and he had her pushed up against the interior wall of the barn. He forced himself on her and raped her against the wall. He belittled her, saying things like "You're so stupid. Why did you do that?" Kathy was in no shape to fight him off. Her tiny body was nothing more than skin and bones. When Paul finished with her, he left her there curled up in a ball on the cold barn floor in tears. He left her to go be with his mistress.

This was a different scene in the lifetime on the large Southern plantation Kathy had visited in the previous session a year before. Although he had moved to the big house, Paul visited Kathy in the cottage from time to time. She was a battered and abused wife. There were bruises on her face that she hid so no one saw, but she was worried about what her daughter knew. He treated her badly, but she continued to protect him.

It hadn't always been this way. Paul and Kathy were happy at first. Although Paul had been controlling, he had also been loving toward her until the death of their young son. Now, from time to time, Paul came by to check on her. When he did, he'd rape her and tell her he loved her, but it was her fault things were this way. If she'd given him a son, he wouldn't have had to be with the other woman. She blamed herself too for not being able to give him a son. He'd rape her, scream terrible things at her, and then leave. This was her way of life now. She'd clean up the blood, cover up the bruises, and act like it never happened...until it happened again.

Kathy's only solace was church. She went there to try to find peace. Paul was shameless in his pursuit to humiliate her. He brought his other family to the same church for Sunday services and paraded them in front of her. His mistress walked past Kathy with her nose in the air while shooting her a disdainful look. People felt sorry for Kathy, but they didn't know what to say. Kathy suffered her embarrassment in silence. She knew if she went against him, she would be left with nothing and nowhere to go because Paul's family was so well connected in the community. Besides, they hadn't done anything to help her or her daughter.

Paul and his mistress didn't have the best relationship either. She treated *him* badly. She spoke down to him, was never satisfied, and ordered him around like a child. He wasn't happy, but he stayed to be with the children. When he'd had enough of that, he'd visit Kathy and take out his frustrations on her. He seemed to enjoy the pain he inflicted upon her.

Kathy had no friends. She spent her time in a rocking chair knitting blankets that she took to the local store to sell. She didn't make much money from them, but it occupied her time. She'd walk to the store where she was met by the nice man who worked there. Kathy recognized him as a close relative in her current life. He showed kindness and concern for her. As he bid her goodbye, he'd give her a hug and say, "Take care of yourself, young lady." This small gesture went a long way in her lonely life.

The cycle of abuse didn't stop; it went on for years. It was a miserable, lonely existence for Kathy. She was tired, worn out, and just couldn't go on like that anymore. Toward the end, Paul couldn't bear to look at Kathy, knowing deep down that he had caused this. He sent for the doctor and asked to be notified with time enough for him to return so she wouldn't be alone when she died. She died of heart-related issues from malnutrition and a broken heart. Kathy welcomed death as a relief. She immediately felt peace at leaving that miserable existence behind.

In the spirit realm, Kathy's spirit is greeted by angelic beings. This time it's a group of females with her male guide situated in the middle. He hugs her and tells her he's so proud of her for all the good work she's done and to keep doing it.

As her guide removes the remaining thread from Kathy that connected her to that lifetime, he tells her she's ready for love now that she's finished doing the emotional work she needed to do. Kathy's mother appears and reminds her that she continues to watch over her. She reassures Kathy she knows how difficult this has been for her. She tells Kathy, "You've suffered with so much loneliness, even in this lifetime, but you won't anymore."

During Soul Reflection, her guide goes over the lessons from that lifetime. He explains that she didn't finish the lesson then, so it carried over into current life, so she could finish it now. He said that "she needed to learn to back away from people who treat her that way."

In her current life she experienced what it was like to be the other woman, so she could gain insight from that perspective. "That's how karma works," he said. "You were the wife before, now you're the mistress. You learned that it's not freer to be the mistress, it's painful, even more so." Kathy realizes why she experienced both sides of it, although neither side of the coin is good. It won't give her the right relationship or the love that she's searching for.

Kathy's mother reassures her that love is coming. She reminds Kathy to have patience and not get frustrated if it's not here today. "Your soul mate has been praying for you too," she says. "It's close to time for us to meet," Kathy confirms. "He's ready and I'm ready. There's nothing else to do."

Kathy says, "She sends me a glimpse of my new love," and adds that "I'll know immediately it's him and he will too." Her guide tells her that's all for now; her spiritual team wants it to be a surprise for her when they meet. Kathy can feel her true love's energy. It leaves her feeling safe, loved, and warm. She's told she'll recognized these feelings when she meets him as a new feeling she hasn't had before in her romantic relationships.

As her current life assessment is winding down, Kathy's guide impresses upon her the need to have more control. "I can control how I react and don't need others to control me," she comments. "I've also noticed a shift in my friendships with others who are toxic and not good for me. He tells me to surround myself with people who are happy, positive, and loving.

I've passed the test of being controlled in relationships. I'm taking my power back and can be truly happy. There's no need to be miserable and abused anymore. I can walk away from that now." Earth is an emotional planet. It's where we come to learn. She's reminded that when we hold the negative emotions in, they come out eventually as illness in the body.

"I'm told it's time for forgiveness," Kathy said. "I can thank Paul for what I learned and release that part of me now. I also need forgiveness of myself. I felt this took too long to learn, but they're telling me it took the time that it took. I had to get it right and experience it." Kathy reveals that her primary lesson in all this has been "learning to love myself. I'm shifting the relationship with myself. And it's making me a better person by taking the shame away." Holding in these negative emotions was toxic to her health.

She went on to explain, "This allows me to be joyful and happy more, and to be around the right people. It's okay to say no! Saying no to someone or something is like saying yes to myself. I need to not be so hard on myself and it's okay to say no! Mom is hugging me, and I feel her support. She's been helping me to figure this out. I'm learning to love myself and to forgive myself."

We end with the symbol of the red heart. Kathy's mother reminds Kathy to focus on the red heart and tells her everything is right on track. Everything is as it was meant to be. Things are taking time because the other players are working out their things too. Have faith, it will happen at the right time. True love finds you no matter where you are...

———— *Soul-Minded Journaling* ————
Shifting Your Relationship with Yourself

If you would like to shift the relationship with yourself, you first need to step back and take a look at yourself objectively. Journal the answers to these questions and look at any patterns you recognize forming with regard to your relationships, friendships, and the people you surround yourself with.

What kinds of people do you surround yourself with? Do they look out for you when you can't look out for yourself, or do they take advantage of your good nature? Are there any toxic people it's time to confront about their behavior or move on from in your life?

Are your relationships honest, loving, and supportive, or are they deceitful, controlling, and demeaning? Do your relationships leave you feeling insecure and doubting yourself? Are you searching for soulful, loving relationships in all the wrong places?

What behaviors in your life are hurtful toward others? Are you the judgmental one in the relationship? Are you supportive of others? Are you flexible or intolerant of the others in your life? Are you honest with the people in your life?

What kind of people do you enjoy spending time with and would like to have more of in your life? Learn to discern love. When it's not right, you know it. Don't settle for less than you deserve. Keep on until you find the right path to manifest the best relationships for your best self to emerge.

—— *Soul-Minded Exercise* ——
Heart Meditation

What does your heart want you to know? Remind you?

Sit quietly, close your eyes. Hand over heart. Breathe. Connect. Feel. Listen. What is your heart guiding you toward? Away from?

If you are confused or aren't clear on what to do next, let the sound of your breathing take you deeper within. As you feel yourself calming, ask your soul or guides, "What would you have me do now?"... and listen. Don't think, just listen. The more you practice, the clearer the answers become and the less time you'll spend in confusion.

chapter 17

Recharge to Inhabit
Your Body More Fully

Cynthia is a spiritually minded individual. She wants a SESR session to connect with her spirit guide and get information about why she has returned to Earth. She finds it difficult to be here at times due to the heaviness of this realm. For some souls, it's difficult for them to fully inhabit their earthly bodies, as is the case for Cynthia. They need time out in nature to get away and ground. As a child, she spent time doing physical activity such as hiking or working out, which helped her to be more present in the body. These sessions give insight into the activities of a soul and why it's more difficult for some to reside in the body as completely as others.

Cynthia goes under quickly and easily as her session begins. Moving along time, she suddenly feels disoriented and begins to weep. She admits she is saed at returning. It is the ninth month of her mother's pregnancy and she dislikes the weight of the heavy feelings in this place and this body, preferring lighter bodies instead because she finds them easier to inhabit.

Cynthia's soul prefers to go higher up, where it's lighter, to where the knowledge and connection to Source are, instead of incarnating on Earth, but she knew she had to. "I thought I was going higher and would stay, I thought that I was done, but a powerful being showed me that I needed to go, my soul needed it...once I knew, I had to," she explains, trying to hold back her tears. Following a series of discussions with her Soul Advisory Council prior to birth, assurances were made to Cynthia and she agreed to incarnate because it was needed for her soul and for the others who would be in her life. They asked her to return, so she did.

Cynthia is pleased with her current body. "She is perfect," she says, describing the body in the third person. It is a strong body. And she knew that with this body she would have the ability to reconnect to a stronger, higher power. Her soul carries a great deal of knowledge that can be overwhelming, making it difficult to break things down quickly in daily life. Adjustments were made to the body during the gestation period to gear it up to connect to the higher frequencies coming though. Light begins pouring in as Cynthia reconnects with these frequencies. A dense, "pure" light, whiter than white, surges through her body like electrical pulses clearing away the dense energies as it pours in, making it difficult for her to talk. Next, she's guided through the darkness to a door framed by a luminescent pink light. As she crosses through the spirit door into the light, instead of moving into an earthly past life she begins to shake and continues to have difficulty speaking because the vibration is so strong. She pops into a lush green landscape, like an ancient garden, but with plants that look different than on Earth. "They're futuristic-looking plants," she says. She feels something between the toes of her bare feet and notices that she's wearing a flowing, robe-like garment of light. Her delicate features are highlighted by her yellow hair and piercing emerald green eyes. She tells me to call her by the name Lilli, which means flower, as she experiences oneness with her soul self. Many arms extend out to Lilli as she is welcomed home by her higher family in this place where the stars, the sun, and souls are connected. She's overwhelmed with emotion, overjoyed at returning.

After a while, a wise being appears. She describes him as Jesus-like, wearing sandals, with a yellow light surrounded by soft blue. His energy is peaceful, very gentle, calm. She tells me he is higher than a guide and "very, very wise." He extends a hand out to Lilli. As his energy touches her, she feels a warmth and a comfort flow through her. She's filled with a knowing that he's here to help her "unfold something on a deeper level."

A series of deep exhalations occur and then a column of strong, yellow light begins pouring in through her third eye. She weeps softly as it pours into her head. It is powerful and bright, moving all the way through her crown and out her feet. A translucent dome covers her third eye, and another is over her heart. The exhalations continue as she releases heavy energies with deep sobs, clearing her emotional body until she begins to feel lighter.

Lilli suddenly feels herself beginning to move. "I'm star traveling...up, up, up...going faster, I can feel the vibration, my body is like a rocket," she says. She has difficulty speaking and shakes, shifting with the vibrations as she moves through the multi-layered spiritual realms. Each vibratory layer creates a ripple effect that is uncomfortable for her dense physical form to adjust to. My client's face visibly contorts as her spirit rockets through the spiritual realms as the rocket itself, as if the g-force is pressing against it. Her voice changes, its sound distorted as if it too is traveling through time and space to reach my ears.

Her many lifetimes quickly flash before her, sparking a remembrance, but with no time for reflection, which isn't necessary anyway. Lilli simultaneously understands what is needed and releases what must be let go as she is embraced by a golden light. She mumbles incoherently finding herself without a body among a field of colors with gorgeous blues, purples, and fuchsia heart-healing energies. Lilli is infused with intense feelings of peace and happiness by other souls coming to send her love. She is guided through an "uplevelment" designed to shift her vibrational level and align her more completely with her higher self.

The wise being returns. His form is "soft, light, pure love." He is to the left of Lilli now sitting on a throne. There's golden brightness around him; pure love permeates as he oversees everybody and everything. I press her to find out more about who this is. She asks if he is really Jesus. He smiles and tells her that he is. Jesus tells her he loves her and thanks her for being strong and doing what she came to do. "Allow yourself to know what you know, don't block," he advises her.

Cynthia now understands that Lilli chose to come back to Earth, although she had completed her incarnations here. She agreed to help with the cosmic shift on Earth at this time to be in service to others. Jesus assures her that it will be okay. He extends his hand and she feels his energy strengthen her. He tells her that trepidation set in in the womb, which he has been clearing during this session. Revisiting this place is to renew her energy, so she can continue with the next phase of this current incarnation. Cynthia's grandmother appears, reminding her that she is strong and that is why she was needed. She tells her to keep going and stay on the path; she will know more in time.

She's joined by two guides. One is a tall, very strong male guide with character. He knows what Lilli is capable of doing and brings her strength during her incarnations, while her softer, fairy-like female guide provides joy. She visits Cynthia often in her daily life as a flash of light, coming across very small and flittery, but powerful.

Lilli's female guide helps her with fantasy, feeling, and escaping by connecting with the light in "the realm before time" where her knowledge flows. Her female guide is from this fairylike place and returns with Lilli whenever she goes there. For Lilli, it's like a reward to get to return here. The ancient garden where she first popped in is a magical realm where Lilli can just fly to whenever she wants to reconnect. Whenever she feels too heavy in her body, she goes there to recharge among the lightness of the flowers and light.

Lilli likes being there very much. This place is home for her soul. Its beautiful light is freeing and she feels connected to everyone and to love. It's a high level with no words; there's a deep understanding of everything and beautiful, supportive energy here. "You just feel these beautiful moments. Everything is just wonderful here." She revels in describing it. "Everything has energy coming from it … the flowers and plants." This place is filled with light energy, magic, and colors not known on Earth. In this place Lilli has wings and can fly.

At this point, Lilli's male guide is somewhere else. His energy is more solid and grounded. Lilli learns a great deal from him. He helps her with lessons regarding her soul direction. "He knows what's best and needs to be completed," she says earnestly. "He says 'sometimes I don't listen.'"

Lilli is a star traveler. It's difficult for her to be in the denseness of the Earth plane. She much prefers to stay in one of the many planes of light. She didn't need to come back to the heaviness, but she came because she knows so much. Her specialty is helping people on their soul journey, but sometimes it's difficult to get them to listen. She helps the ones she can, but it can be difficult to connect with them, unlike at "home" where everyone is connected already. "There's none of that hardness or being busy with words to try to figure it out...you just already know," Lilli explains. On Earth she first has to figure out how others can connect to what she's trying to tell them, so she can help them. It feels so good when she can get through to them, which reminds her of that feeling of being connected at home. "You know they get it. You can see it and feel it, but it's very hard...very rare," she explains.

Lilli asks if she's on track in her present life. Her guides remind her that it's not how many you help, it's what you do with the ones who are sent. Her knowledge is needed and she's to share from the heart. She's made aware of a feeling she gets, a different kind of energy that comes over her when "higher knowledge" comes out. The heart is the connection. She's assured she's on the right path now; the work she's doing is helping others to connect to information they need. Her guides clap for her, celebrating her accomplishments, revealing it is her male guide who nudged her to the "chair" for today's session.

He reveals that Jesus is Lilli's higher source, a master teacher higher than a guide and higher than an archangel. He speaks to the hierarchy in the highest realms of the spirit world as levels and lighter layers going higher up. Lilli is aware of colors of darker blues and purples contained in a vastness that can be felt when getting as close as one is allowed to go. There are different levels of guides, and higher guides with intellect and higher knowledge, including the Soul Advisory Council, who are wise and powerful mentors for humans.

In addition, there are healers and angelic beings who have strong energies. Some angels such as archangels work with humans, while a special group of very powerful angels work with certain beings (non-incarnate) at higher levels. Their information is very guarded and not for humans or even some levels of guides to know. Jesus and other master teachers reside between the levels of archangels and the specialty angels who work with Source. I press further and am told it's not for "humans to know."

Higher than guides and healers but lower than the specialty angels and master teachers are the souls of special pets, horses, and beautiful animals (including unicorns). Animals are so high up because their spirits are pure. Not all animals have this spirit, but some do.

As you go up through the layers, there's collective knowledge. At the highest level is Source, a brilliant light so blinding and an energy so powerful. "We know that light, we know we're naturally attracted to that light, we're heading, all of us, heading in that direction. Some take a lot longer to feel it there, but it's there," Lilli said.

Next, she is visited by her special pets who have crossed over. Her male guide reveals that her special pets are sent to her from her home to bring her joy. When things get too heavy, she can escape in the woods for a walk with them to remind her it's only temporary here. Pets are energy balancers. They help us to relieve tension and stress of our earthly lives. When we are too out of balance, it causes them to take on too much and they begin to get the same illness patterns as their owners. Her guides reveal to her the ways they help her release tension and stress. They use humor and joy to lift her up when she needs a lift. They remind her to bring hope and joy back with her.

Cynthia's session ends here. She's left with a lot to take in as this knowledge is reawakened within her. It has been an intense couple of hours, with many strong vibrational shifts carried along with the light as she traveled through the various layers of the realms. She laughs, commenting that her session wasn't all "light and floaty" as her friend's session had been. I explain that for some, the experience is more intense than for others. And although she expected to explore her past lives, her spiritual team had a plan of their own.

She admits she's surprised that Jesus is her master teacher. She considers herself spiritual, but not religious. Even as a child, she had naturally been drawn toward Eastern thought instead of the Christian-based religions, finding a special interest in martial arts.

(As an aside, typically when clients see a being who shows up appearing to be Jesus, I ask them to take a closer look. When they do, it often turns out to be their guide instead. In this session with Cynthia, the energy was palpable in the room and his presence was of a much brighter and more powerful light than that of a guide. The planet she visited is the "Orange Planet" many souls speak of. Its hue is like the color of the sunset or a Himalayan salt lamp which is calming to souls of this origin. It's her soul's joyful planet/place. There's water there too. On Earth she uses water, sunsets, and the beautiful orangey glow of a Himalayan salt lamp as tools for rebalancing, healing, and comfort.)

Knowing that she's found her way through some difficult times yet is still on her spiritual path is reassuring to Cynthia.

She feels stronger with the knowledge that she has moved past her fears and found her way through all of that, acquiring new skills as a result. She's reminded of that sense of knowing that hits her in the heart, and she knows she's to trust it and to act on it when it does.

After an intense session, Cynthia needs quiet time to process all that she's experienced. She finds it on the beach, listening to the waves roll in as the sun sets over the water.

—— Soul-Minded Exercise ——
Connecting to Your Body

We all need a break from our daily life, to take time out to recharge. Physical activity such as hiking, walking, dance, yoga, breath work, biking, swimming, surfing, martial arts, kayaking, skiing, working out—even singing—are great activities for de-stressing and freeing your spirit. Taking time out for a beautiful sunset is a great punctuation mark to the end of the day.

Music can lift you up and raise your vibration. Clear space in the middle of the room. Put on your favorite dance music and let your spirit dance. Dance it out!

Feel a renewal, a sense of freedom returning as you release heavy energies. Feel yourself getting lighter and becoming more present in your body.

What are some of the ways you recharge to inhabit your body more fully?

Conclusion

In conclusion, it is my hope that in reading these stories of healing, you are able to put your own fears to rest as a result of finding answers to questions you have had about the spiritual realms. Know that your soul is being guided daily and constantly. Fear hinders your ability to be present in your life and to be in touch with messages from your spiritual team. May the practical exercises help you expand your connection to your soul and guides by helping you realign your focus with their guidance and a new perspective that connects you to your soulfulness.

Soul guidance does not come from the thinking mind; the way in is through the heart. Opening the heart opens access to the soul's wisdom. In doing so, you can resolve longstanding issues to find a sense of peace within yourself. My clients have benefited from amazing SESR revelations that led to the release of anger, sadness, fear, and guilt. Following a SESR session, you can then return to a more joyful state aligned with your soul and your life's purpose, with a deeper understanding of yourself and your place in this world. With this self-knowledge, you feel supported knowing that life is not a random series of events and you are not alone in your human existence. You are able to know you belong. More aware of who you truly are, you can go where you are meant to best shine your light with confidence, knowing you are already on the right path.

With an understanding that there is a bigger plan in place during your incarnations, my hope is for you to recognize your uniqueness in contributing to humanity as the limitless soul that you are, in the way that only you can.

Glossary

Guide: A spiritual being who assists souls with their earthly lessons while they remain in contact with us from the spirit world. Guides focus on the details to get the job done. A guide may stay with a soul throughout many lifetimes. There may be more than one guide. Each has a specialty they assist us with.

Rest and rejuvenation: This is done upon entry into the spirit world following a past life to clear negative imprints or heaviness from the past life.

Soul Advisory Council: A group of wise beings who are not incarnate. They assist souls in prelife planning and oversee a soul's incarnations. The Soul Advisory Council focuses on the big picture in creating the environment for the soul's growth. They are higher in evolution than a guide. Also known as Elders, Wise Beings, the Wise Ones, Sages.

Soul Awareness area: This area holds detailed self-knowledge about a soul, such as their immortal name, soul characteristics, and soul's purpose throughout *all* of their lifetimes.

Soul groups: The group of souls that incarnate together in various roles to assist one another with their lessons and experiences.

Soul mate: The primary member of one's soul group that we incarnate with, like no other, whose soul was created at the same time as ours. A one-of-a-kind soul whose love for their soul mate is unconditional.

Soul Recalibration: When a client receives a powerful download of their soul's energy that helps them to align more completely with their soul's energy, for a stronger connection to soul for the next stages of their life.

Soul Reflection area: This area is where a soul reviews details of their soul's history with regard to their past, future, and current lives with their guide.

Soul Recognition: This occurs during the past life or during Soul Reflection when someone from a client's present life appears in their past life. This is possible because a portion of one's soul remains in the spirit world while one is incarnate.

Spirit world: The realm in the afterlife that souls return to upon death. Also referred to as cosmic realms or heaven.

Spiritual team: Consists of Soul Advisory Council and guides that are assigned to souls to oversee and assist them while incarnating.

To Write to the Author

If you wish to contact the author or would like more information about this book, please write to the author in care of Llewellyn Worldwide Ltd. and we will forward your request. Both the author and publisher appreciate hearing from you and learning of your enjoyment of this book and how it has helped you. Llewellyn Worldwide Ltd. cannot guarantee that every letter written to the author can be answered, but all will be forwarded. Please write to:

Bryn Blankinship
℅ Llewellyn Worldwide
2143 Wooddale Drive
Woodbury, MN 55125-2989

Please enclose a self-addressed stamped envelope for reply,
or $1.00 to cover costs. If outside the U.S.A., enclose
an international postal reply coupon.

Many of Llewellyn's authors have websites with additional information and resources. For more information, please visit our website at http://www.llewellyn.com.